THE 39

TO A RICH

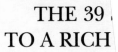

About the Author

Paul Banfield has worked in the financial services industry for 20 years. A qualified Independent Financial Adviser, and director of a large, successful company, Paul is renowned for his no-nonsense, jargon-free advice and has been named 'The Money GP' by the public and media alike. He is consulted regularly as an expert commentator by large organizations such as Cahoot and the Department for Work and Pensions. His articles are published in major national newspapers and magazines and he frequently appears on live and recorded broadcasts for the BBC, ITN, Sky, Channel 4, and CNN, helping viewers to understand the latest financial developments.

THE 39 STEPS
TO A
RICH FUTURE

Paul Banfield

RIGHT WAY

Constable & Robinson Ltd
3 The Lanchesters
162 Fulham Palace Road
London W6 9ER
www.right-way.co.uk
www.constablerobinson.com

First published by Right Way,
an imprint of Constable & Robinson, 2009

A copy of the British Library Cataloguing in Publication
Data is available from the British Library

ISBN: 978-0-7160-2195-7

Printed and bound in the EU

1 3 5 7 9 10 8 6 4 2

ACKNOWLEDGEMENTS

My deep thanks go to the following people who have all played a huge part in who I am and what I have achieved so far; without whom this book would have been a whole different story.

Daphne Himmel for being so clever and wise. Tracy McNamara who is almost as enthusiastic as I am (I love enthusiastic!). Zoe Denny who is simply the best PA ever. Edd and Will Banfield (my two sons) who are big stars! Irene and Phil who give me life, and I love life . . . Jake (my stepson) who is also a star. Petrina Brown (my little sister) because she is brilliant and, as a published author, a great help. Peter (my brother) who is such a nice person and supports my media work. All the people I have worked with on TV and in the media who seem to like my 'straight to the point comments'. My wonderful staff at Best Advice Financial Planning, including my fellow director Tony Moss and also Tracey Murphy for all the extra hours as and when needed. My clients who are a joy to work with and great to know. Finally, to a special lady called Roses, who I am sure will read this book one day . . .

INTRODUCTION

Let's face facts; most of us want to be well-off. There are a few who claim that money isn't important and they may quote the old cliché about money not buying love or happiness, but I think they're trying to comfort themselves because they believe, as is very likely, that they will live a lifetime of not having enough money, of worrying about interest rate rises and inflation and non-existent pensions . . .

The basic truth is that most people would, at the very least, like to be comfortable and free from the day-to-day financial worries which place such a burden on many lives. A record number of people petitioned for bankruptcy during 2007; over 53,000 in England and Wales could not cope with their spiralling debts. This figure is set to rocket as the recession deepens. Unmanageable debt is often kept secret from family and friends and the mounting pressure leads some people to end their lives. Some people turn to gambling. While some of this is frittered away by the mega-rich who simply don't know what to do with all their cash, an awful lot is risked by people desperate for a way to make easy money.

The bad news (let's get it out of the way first) is that the majority of people scrape through their whole lives and live on a miserly pension at the end of thirty or possibly forty years of work. Young people mortgage themselves to the hilt simply to get on the first rung of the property ladder; a feat which is increasingly difficult to achieve. All in all just getting by is a bit of a battle.

Time for the good news! It doesn't have to be like that. Whatever your age or financial position there is a way forward, onward, upwards even in the middle of an economic downturn. By following some of my basic rules you can turn your situation around in a relatively short space of time and simply choose wealth rather than poverty.

If you long for any or all of the following, then this book is perfect for you. To:

- Own your own home
- Be free of crippling mortgage payments
- Look forward to a comfortable retirement
- Treat family and friends
- Enjoy holidays whenever and wherever you choose
- Privately educate your children
- Dine at the top restaurants
- Spend whatever and whenever without guilty feelings
- Pay off debts including credit cards

All you have to do is decide now that you are ready to commit to the 39 steps that will take you to a better, more prosperous and stress-free life. I will show you how it is possible to become free of debt (if you have any) and start using your money to make money rather than staying trapped in a cycle of poverty (many people never break free of this). By following the rules of the rich I guarantee your life will improve. If you are ready to commit to the 39 steps I will reveal to you:

- How to break free of all debt
- How to begin making money
- How to use that money to make more money
- How to invest the money you make
- How to hang on to it

And, most important of all…

- How to enjoy it

At this point you may be thinking to yourself, 'It's not possible for me, my situation is different,' and that's OK, it's best to deal with any negative thoughts before you set off on the road that leads to my 39 steps because once you begin you have to be 100 per cent committed.

You may think that you have restrictions in your life, obstacles that seem simply too difficult to overcome. Perhaps you lack a decent education or have young children who absorb a great deal of your time and energy. These things will not prevent you from climbing the steps that will lead you to wealth and prosperity; paradoxically, they will make the climb all the sweeter and your accomplishments even more satisfying. Barriers can be used as stepping stones. It's all about choice. Let me tell you about myself . . .

When I was a child I was school-phobic; I wouldn't go to school. I don't mean I was an awkward kid who just didn't want to go. I mean I felt trapped and stifled inside the school building, almost claustrophobic, but as soon as I escaped those walls I made a full recovery. Consequently I didn't stay on at school any longer than I had to and didn't enjoy the benefits of a college education. Some people would assume then that I would be doomed to failure in dead-end jobs with little hope of achieving much in life.

But I was always told, from a very young age, that anything

is possible if you want it enough. I think that's partly why I 'chose' to be successful. I had a very strong sense of purpose and refused to fall at any hurdles I came across. I was persistent and unyielding and my mind was never very far from my dream of making a success in business.

I started out at sixteen without a penny to my name but I *knew* that I would find a way to success. Mark Twain pointed out that, 'All you need in this life is ignorance and confidence and then success is sure', and I believe this to be true. I had, in fact, one of the few things that money can't buy: I was hungry for success. I had nothing to lose, nothing to live up to, only my own dogged determination and utter and total confidence that I would succeed with my ambition. And I did. I now own one of the most successful financial companies in the UK and enjoy the profits of my hard work, living my life to the full.

I'm not saying it was easy and all of a sudden I was rich. Certainly not, I have worked hard at it. But I didn't like not having any money and was confident that I would like having it very much indeed. I chanced my arm a few times, did jobs I would rather not have done (though nothing illegal I hasten to add) and worked damned hard at everything I did. Despite this I thoroughly enjoyed this period of my life; hard work is good for the soul! Initially, while first building my business I stayed up half the night driving a cab and spent weekends painting and decorating for extra money. I dedicated many hours to study to gain qualifications I had missed from my school days and used these to assist me in my quest to move onwards and upwards to specific financial qualifications.

My determination increased as I watched my business growing to the point where I could concentrate solely on that alone, and knowing that my income was created by the fruits of my own labour gave me a huge buzz and renewed my zeal to become more successful. I decided at the age of 16 to leave school and become a self-made man and within ten years I had achieved my goal.

So why have I chosen to write this book? Firstly, I am an expert in the field of money. Since the age of 16 I have studied money; my time off was spent studying and I gained specialist financial qualifications needed to set me on my chosen path. I had not a penny of capital but needed it to set up my own business so I learnt how to get hold of it as quickly as possible. I learnt the art of making it grow and I gained immense satisfaction in every little step I took. I made a few bad decisions but I learnt from those and, anyway, each error renewed my pertinacity.

Secondly, I know I can help anyone to become wealthy – anyone. I am not only sharing my thoughts, ideas and experience of becoming a businessman in the hope that my observations will help others to fulfil their own ambitions. I have changed my own life and I have helped many clients to achieve their financial goals too. The fact is that making people wealthy is my business. Yes, I have technical expertise gained from study and experience but I also have a flair for turning bad situations around; no matter how tricky things appear I help people to create healthy and thriving financial credentials. That's how I have become known as 'The Money GP'.

My company, Best Advice Financial Planning Ltd, is a market-leading countrywide financial services company offering holistic expert financial advice including Inheritance Tax planning, retirement planning, investment and saving advice, debt counselling and mortgage protection. I know the money markets and that knowledge helps me to make money fast.

And I am confident I can help you do the same. I want to share what I have learnt and help you become rich. As it happens I have a feeling that I would nevertheless be enjoying my life even if I were still poor since getting pleasure out of life has more to do with attitude than anything else and I have a very positive attitude. But dining at the Ritz whenever I feel like it and staying in some of the most beautiful hotel rooms in the world whenever I go travelling definitely makes life more enjoyable and I'm certainly glad to be in a position to do all of this.

So what's the secret? Can it all simply be down to choice? The answer to that is yes. Wealth and poverty have long been a part of human tapestry; some of our ancestors used their strength and skills to gain dominance and power over others. All we can do is hypothesize as to the secrets of their success; how and why some were able to rise above the rest. But I'll wager a guess that those who achieved great things possessed an inner drive and determination that others lacked. It has been suggested by economists that if all the money in the world were gathered together and redistributed in equal shares to everyone on the earth, it would eventually end up in the pockets of the original owners. They accept the inevitable inequality in life and the natural dominance that some people possess.

We all know people like this, those who appear to have mastered the trick of enjoying an easy life. They breeze through the years with enough money and confidence to overcome any hurdles they come across. Then there are others who, frankly, find it all a bit of a struggle.

This book is designed for those who, so far, haven't found it all that easy. Profitable situations just haven't fallen into their lap the way it seems they do for some. By following the sound financial guidance in this book I will help you achieve all you wish for, simply by choosing to do so. What's more, I'm going to show you how to do it legally and without upset or inconvenience to anyone else. You won't need to become ruthless, you won't need to bully anyone and you certainly don't need to compromise your morals. You can even help others along the way as you climb, by being a fair, encouraging and positive colleague/partner/boss. There are people who have acquired their wealth by being ruthless, dictatorial bullies who aren't afraid to compromise their morals and being basically pretty unpleasant to work with/for. Gaining wealth by devious means or by being a bully negates all the pleasure it offers. Assuming you want to sleep at night and enjoy the profits of your efforts without climbing over others on your way up, I will show you the way to wealth by honest means.

I'm not saying it's going to be easy. If turning your finances around and becoming wealthy was a doddle I would have called this book *Fast-track to Wealth* or *Get Rich Quick* or something equally evocative to draw in the crowds like the myriad of other titles available these days. But the fact is that making real money requires discipline, dedication and sheer hard work (sorry). If you're looking for an easy option I suggest you take your chances in the casino; some will win, most will lose. If you want to get rich by legal means and you're not afraid of hard work it's time to begin the journey. Let's walk out of the shadow of being poor. Join me on the first step to a rich future.

And, remember, you can be rich. It's simply an attitude of mind. Let me show you a better way.

PART ONE

GETTING INTO THE MINDSET OF MONEY

STEP 1

START BELIEVING

Our destiny is shaped by our thoughts and our actions.
We cannot direct the wind but we can adjust the sails.
Anonymous

Anyone can be wealthy. It's simply a case of applying yourself. That is the lesson behind Step 1 – the tricky part is learning to believe it; learning to believe that you are destined for great things. Hopefully by the end of this step you will be fully confident that what you aim for is achievable with hard work and determination. But before we go any further I think it's a good idea to examine a few important issues:

- What you think about wealth
- Your feelings towards wealthy people
- Your reasons for wanting to be wealthy

The reason it is wise to deal with this first is that some people have guilty feelings about acquiring wealth. They feel, or perhaps they have been raised to think, that *the love of money is the root of all evil*. Conditioned thoughts like these *can* last a lifetime, but you don't have to let them. That's one of the best things about taking control – from now on YOU decide on the direction to go, no one else.

I was raised as a Jehovah's Witness and have had many beliefs 'drilled' into me since infancy including constant negative connotations with wealth such as the words of warning found in the Book of Matthew in the Bible: 'It is easier for a camel to go through the eye of a needle, than for a rich man to enter into the Kingdom of God.' I believe it is the person within that is judged and not how wealthy they have become; good can be found in both rich and poor alike.

Some preach that the pursuit of material things is a desire born of greed and corruption. I accept that the idolisation of money is not a healthy pastime, but my pursuit of money has been a very positive one! I don't lust after money itself. It doesn't define me. Money hasn't compromised my sincerity. I'm not a man who sits alone in the evenings with my cash, diligently counting to make sure I have enough.

Some people sneer at those who have accumulated wealth, as if it's something to be ashamed of. Do I feel guilty? NO! All I want to do is share what I have learnt in my climb to success. I want to offer you a passport to a better world, the world I now inhabit, and, yes, it is so much nicer than the one I was in. Maybe you're thinking, 'So what if you can afford to shop at Harrods? What's so great about flying first class? Are you really happier Paul, staying in a five-star hotel instead of a run-of-the-mill guesthouse? Does it really make a difference to see a doctor at your convenience, is the grass really greener?' The answer is a big 'YES! Come and taste it! Yes, it makes a difference. Yes, I'm happier and yes, it has a lot do with money.'

There are also people, I even know a few myself, who fear losing their money to the extent that their life is over-shadowed, dominated by that fear. Their wealthy souls are tormented by the fear and insecurity that it could all be gone tomorrow. For them being rich is a poisoned chalice. They fear the loss of what they own to the point that they can't enjoy what they have. I think it's very sad but it doesn't mean that money, or the desire for ownership of it, is always negative, any more than, with alcoholics in the world, the love of a good wine is a bad thing. I think that in order to move further along the path to prosperity all negative associations have to be cast aside. What you must do very early on in your climb, preferably now, is to set yourself free from the constraints that others place on you.

You *must* overcome any ingrained fears and insecurities about being successful as you may face a backlash. I am bewildered that here in the UK it seems a majority of people always like the underdog and just love to hate a winner. I have always decided against following the herd; it's best to be a shepherd and not a sheep I was always told as a child! And the result is a richer, happier me. I thoroughly enjoy having money but that doesn't mean it rules me. It certainly doesn't. I wouldn't say I'm greedy either. I just prefer having money to being poor, simple as that. I don't believe my integrity is compromised. I have remained close to all my family and friends (however, they all adore Christmas more these days!).

Some people may tell you that you'll end up sacrificing your principles and losing your friends in your clamour to be rich but it doesn't have to be like that. You can still be a socialist, if that is your political leaning, and have money. You can retain your sense of humour and your friends, as well as taking the occasional day off. You can believe in equality and opportunity for all, be spiritual, enjoy good morals and be honest in all your dealings. You may even find yourself in a position where you can do a whole lot of good with the wealth you've acquired (see Step 38), not just for yourself and for your family but for worthy causes you feel strongly about.

If you feel half-hearted or concerned about the effect wealth may have on your character, then sub-consciously you weaken your determination to succeed. What I'm saying is that you have to be confident that the end result of all your efforts will be a worthwhile one, not just financially but in all aspects of your life. If, as you work your way up the steps you find you're having very little fun, I suggest you stop climbing. Forget the plan and do something you enjoy. If you have to lie and cheat, defraud, break the law in any way, lose sleep or upset others, it won't make you happy (hopefully) if you can't look at yourself in the mirror.

If you worry that you can't be both ethical and rich let me reassure you. I have twenty-two years' experience in the industry of finance. I have met and worked with people from many different backgrounds and circumstances. The only thing I have found that my wealthy clients all have in common is that they've all worked their socks off to achieve it, apart from the *lucky* (in italics because I think it is far more rewarding, satisfying and appreciated if it's been hard to come by and strived for) few who have inherited, won or married it.

Before you are ready to move on to Step 2 you must have discarded any negative thoughts or ingrained beliefs that may hold you back and stand in the way of your new life. Get rid of them, purge them and maximize your chances of achieving your goal. Negative feelings and thoughts didn't get the telephone invented or devise the theory behind the big bang and, 'No pessimist ever discovered the secret of the stars, or sailed to an uncharted land, or opened a new doorway for the human spirit,' in the words of Helen Keller.

So why do you want to be wealthy? How will you know when you're wealthy enough? What will you do with it once you've amassed it? These are all questions you should ponder. It will take a huge amount of time and dedication to get there – if you feel you'd rather spend the time bumming around doing very little, then this quest is not for you. I want you to bear in mind that once you have a large amount of money it won't ever be large enough to buy back the years you've spent getting there. No man will ever be rich enough to do that. Consider whether you are hungry enough for it. Make up your mind to accept a few knocks that you will almost certainly experience along the way . . .

Once you make up your mind and start believing that you have the power to achieve great things, the rest will follow. Unswerving self-belief and total self-assurance are priceless attributes, almost more important than any other skill or knowledge you may possess. Winston Churchill had enough of both to instil unconquerable attitudes and belief in our entire nation and this undoubtedly contributed to altering the course of our history. Start believing in yourself and the power of wanting something badly enough and then you are ready to explode from the blocks!

A few pointers to remember from this first step:

- There are good and bad people, some rich, some poor
- You are in control; YOU decide how rich you want to be
- YOU decide what to do with your wealth
- Money can do an awful lot of good
- Wealth is out there for the taking – believe in your ability and be positive
- Blind faith and optimism go a long way

I'd rather be a could-be if I cannot be an are,
Because a could-be is a maybe who is reaching for a star,
I'd rather be a has-been than a might-have-been by far,
For a might-have-been has never been but a has-been
was once an are . . .
Milton Berle

STEP 2

START NOW; IT'S NEVER
TOO LATE

The only thing that can console one for being poor is extravagance.
Oscar Wilde

A common assumption many people make is that all the chances in life have passed them by. If a house, career or prosperity hasn't come their way in their twenties they sit back and think, 'Oh dear, it's too late now'. Firstly, this is often used as an excuse for doing nothing; that old chestnut *laziness* rearing its ugly head again! And, secondly, it's never ever too late to make a difference or 'be who you might have been' in the words of George Eliot. Resist the urge to slip into apathy. Old age beckons those without enthusiasm for life and all of its many possibilities. No matter what your age you can go out there and conquer your own little bit of the world.

Yes, life is short. Time is the enemy. And once we reach a certain age it can be difficult to make dramatic changes. But you can renew (or perhaps cultivate for the first time) your vigour for life. And you chose this book for a reason. My hunch is that you are not wholly satisfied with your lot at the moment. Well, I'm very glad you chose to act when you did and I'm pleased to be taking you on this journey with me. What I'm offering is not a magic bullet that will solve all of life's problems overnight, but a solid strategy that will, if you follow it carefully, resolve the financial issues in your life and will even have a domino effect in other areas where you are perhaps dissatisfied. Did you know for example, that business and financial success can have a marked effect on your libido? It's true. By Step 9 or 10 you should be noticing a difference . . .

May I suggest that you only tell your nearest and dearest about your plans to make changes in your life, changes that will bring you great rewards? In fact, if you don't think they'll be positive about it don't even tell them (particularly the bit about the likely changes in your libido, unless you know this will receive a positive response!). Well, not until you have to at least. They may not be as supportive as you'd like them to be. You may find you are bombarded with endless examples of people who have tried to 'better themselves' in the past and have 'fallen flat on their face'. Others listening in who are equally disappointed with the way their life has panned out will agree, moving their heads like nodding dogs. Bear in mind that many people meet their downfall by trying to please too many people and never pleasing themselves. Don't fall prey to others who try to place restrictions on you.

You may find that friends and family are even bothered enough by your plans to call you a fool. Don't listen to them. Turn away from negative hot air; it's so counter-productive. You'll only run out of chances when you stop looking for them. You don't have to be a young whipper-snapper in order to make positive changes in your life; youth is wasted on the young after all.

Negative opinions and vacuous remarks of the envious, ignorant or plain lazy brigade should spur you on all the more.

So read on my patient friend, we will get there in good time, sooner than you think. And there can be positives to starting later in life. You probably have more patience and pertinacity than your junior counterparts and, 'being young is greatly overrated. Any failure seems so total. Later on, you realize you can have another go,' a point made by the fashion designer Mary Quant.

Make up your mind not to drag your feet. If you ponder on it too long you will no doubt come up with one hundred and one different reasons not to do anything. Let's not waste any more time. You won't get rich that way. If you're reading this book in bed I want you to wake the next morning with action in your mind. If not tomorrow, then when will you get round to it? When things have settled down in your life? Once your kids have left school? When you have saved a few more pennies in your low interest savings account? What are you waiting for?

Forgive yourself your lack of action so far in life. Put it behind you. But don't be so forgiving in the future. Don't let the petty distractions in life or a lack of impetus prevent you from achieving the things you dreamed of as a teenager. 'If onlys' won't be much consolation as you sit in your nursing home when you're 90. However, a glass of the finest Chablis Grand Cru that money can buy and the prettiest nurse might help. Inside yourself you just know there lay an impulsive trait that can barely wait to be unleashed, an inner drive you've ignored or at least perhaps turned the volume down on. Stall no more, my hard-working friend. Don't accept mediocre for a minute longer. START NOW.

It's never too late. Accept that, inwardly digest it and believe it without reservation. If you think it's too late, then it will be. You may as well hang up your boots right now. The game will be over before it's begun. The path is blocked; the way ahead is not open to you. If you appreciate that there are boundless opportunities open to you, then the waters will part and allow you to make your way through. Trust me, work with me and let's start the journey together.

I see many new clients who have not bothered to make financial plans because they hit 30 and feel it's too late. They even put pension plans on the back-burner because they feel they should have started in their 20s and now there is just no point. Likewise, many people stagnate in boring, unfulfilling, soul-destroying jobs because it's the path they set out on when they left school/college/university and they feel it's too late for change.

The fact is that making successful changes is not dictated by age or any other factors except motivation and determination. Some people feel that their whole life experience is commanded, verbatim, by the situation they were catapulted into at birth and that their own actions have very little to do with it. But it has everything to do with it – *everything*. This book is the tool you need to unlock a focused determination that will lead to super-abundance. Knowledge is a powerful tool in the right hands – I have the knowledge and I'm handing you the power, NOW.

Shift your focus, don't drift through the next week/month/years – choose a new path and head off first thing tomorrow. Alter your course and take yourself in a different direction; then it won't matter how long you've been headed the wrong way.

Be ready to duck and dive a little, not in an Arthur Daley dodgy dealing kind of way. I mean in a being ready-for-anything, flexible way. Loosen your shackles. Be open to doing things differently. If doing what you've always done hasn't yet propelled you into a life of abundance, then I suggest it's time to do something a bit different. After all, even Del Boy 'made it' in the end . . . (I know he went on to lose it but he did achieve his dream of being a millionaire.)

Approaching your quest for plenitude in this way will hopefully renew your vigour for life as well. Opening your mind will not only free your thinking for opportunities to build wealth but may also encourage you to see life as an adventure and a chance perhaps to widen your circle of friends, expanding your horizons at the same time.

I'm not suggesting that if you choose to follow a different path the universe will acknowledge your desires, appreciate that you deserve it, and somehow cosmically transform your life without any effort or hard work (as some recent publications seem to suggest!). But deciding on your new path is an important and vital first step. It's also often the most difficult.

And, of course, you will face many challenges along the way. But who said life wouldn't throw a few obstacles in your path and then a few more for good measure?! The trick is to keep at it with unswerving persistence; view each and every setback as a spur to make you stronger and more determined. At the very least, having financial freedom will allow you to explore the world in a way that was not possible before, if nothing else.

- Remember, doing what you've always done will only get you what you've always had.

Obviously I would advise prudence from a very early age (see Step 10) but it's not the end of the world if you learn these lessons a little later in life. How much longer are you prepared to wait for fate to lay its hands on you? Do you think that someone else is going to come along at some point in your life and give you a helping hand? You're living in a fool's paradise; no one is coming. You're out there on your own. Are you willing to lay yourself on the line? Will you dare to try? You have to be willing to make a few sacrifices. It's not a mission for the faint of heart. Aren't you eager to pull aside the veil of failure and take a peak at the success concealed behind? Don't be afraid. Everyone deserves to try another bite of the cherry, don't they? What's to stop you?

Remember:

- It's never too late
- Ignore moaners and whiners
- The only barrier against success is yourself
- Vanquish your fears
- Go out and conquer a small piece of the world for yourself; it's there waiting for you to stamp your name on it . . .
- Time to shift gear into *hyper-drive*

We'll set off on your endeavour for riches together, join me!

STEP 3

MOTIVATE YOURSELF TO RICHES

Mon cher, practically speaking, I know everything!
Hercule Poirot

If you want to be rich you have to sit and think about it. Think about wealth and motivate yourself to the point where you have to do something about it. Getting motivated is not only the most difficult part of the journey but also one of the most important steps you will take on the road to success. Some people are naturally more motivated than others.

If you took an assorted bunch of people and arranged for them to be shipwrecked on a remote island (a crazy suggestion I know but it would be an interesting social experiment), it would soon sort the wheat from the chaff in terms of levels of personal motivation; some would spring into action and others would be more than happy to sit back and see what materialized. The motivated would hunt for food and strive to build shelter, planning for the long haul while hoping for rescue. Others would give in to their fate, waiting around and wishing that sustenance would materialize; not actually doing anything constructive and just hoping that things would be all right.

We all know people like this, who can't motivate themselves to find their way out of a paper bag, let alone a primitive island. But you can't survive on a desert island by sitting back and hoping that what you need will come to you and, likewise, you can't make money by wishing for it. You can't become wealthy by being lazy.

Bear in mind that:

- Nobody creates wealth by being lazy
- Now is the time for change
- No one is going to do it for you
- Work like your life depends on it
- A will finds a way (Orison Swett Marden)

Millionaires find a way. They start out with enormous drive and ambition. They have long-term goals. They are prepared to forgo instant gratification for long-term success. They get out of bed earlier than most and know what they want to achieve. They demonstrate self-control and never blame anyone else for their own failings or inactivity.

I have a friend whose husband suffers from symptoms caused by idleness. He is forever moaning and griping about their circumstances and lack of money. He 'blames' his stagnation on:

- The fact that they married early
- They had children too young
- They overstretched themselves on their first mortgage
- His parents
- Her parents
- His boss

- His teachers
- Anyone else he can think of

I have only had the misfortune to chat to him a couple of times (I'm afraid I have very low tolerance levels when it comes to doom-mongers) but each of those times he concluded the conversation with, 'It's all right for you because . . . ' and then went on to say that everything happened to fall into my lap, I had the 'Midas Touch', etc, while he's never been lucky enough to win a goldfish! I blame his affliction on no one but himself. I have nothing against laziness, only people who are lazy and have the cheek to whinge about it – MOVE ON!

Others blame their circumstances on bad luck. They gripe on about always having the misfortune of being in the wrong place at the wrong time. I'd like a golden nugget for every time I've heard someone moan when a new invention hits the market crying, 'I had that idea years ago, why do I never benefit?' Think about it, matey! Horses for courses, I say. You did nothing to make your idea a reality, you made no effort, sat back and waited for someone else to put all the hard work in and now you want a piece of the pie?! Fortune only favours the brave!

I love the German word *schadenfreude*. Translated it means harm-joy, a malicious enjoyment of another's misfortune. It describes perfectly the state of mind of those hearse chasers who find pleasure in other people's misery. They don't like to hear about people doing well. They don't want to hear good news – it puts them in an even worse mood. A bit like the rubber-necks who slow down on the motorway to see the aftermath of an accident or those who are constantly miserable until they hear a bit of bad news, then they suddenly liven up.

I had my very own prophet of doom working for my company a few years ago. He was never happy unless someone had a problem; as soon as he heard a nugget of bad news he would suddenly become all animated and lively. I tolerated his bad attitude for many months but his negativity was so ubiquitous that there seemed to be a little black cloud floating not only over his desk but around the entire office. I decided to sack him and immediately boosted staff morale, filling the office with rays of warmth. It cheered everyone up and gave him something genuine to moan about so, all in all, I think I did him a favour. He went through life expecting bad luck and it's exactly what he got.

However, I have to say that one of the teachings I agree with from my staunchly religious background is the conviction held by religious institutions that there is no such thing as luck, whether it be good or bad. Many people find superstitions ridiculous in the twenty-first century but it seems that most subscribe to the 'good luck/bad luck theory'. The truth is you make your own luck. The pagan gods of misfortune are figments of the imagination, in my book. Good fortune comes to those who earn it. Grab chances when you see them and don't let go until you pull yourself up from the place you find yourself in and find your new direction.

It can be difficult to accept that the buck stops with you and no one else. I believe that many people secretly hope that someone will come and improve their life for them. I even think it is a factor that influences extra-marital affairs and relationship break-ups; a new relationship offers the enticement of a different and possibly better life. It can be daunting to acknowledge it's probably not going to happen unless we ourselves do something to make it happen. As Goethe put it, 'I have come to the frightening conclusion that I am the decisive element . . . It is my daily mood that makes the weather. I possess tremendous power to make life miserable or joyous.' Once you accept the inevitable, that success is a dividend of sweat, you can take the steps you need to make a better life.

However difficult you think it may be or whatever life has thrown at you so far, now is the time to change things. The self-motivated person springs into action no matter how difficult his or her circumstances; in the words of Nelson Mandela, 'the greater part of our happiness or misery depends on our character and not our circumstances'.

Bad times may come but remember that they pass. Let them wash over you. View life as a work in progress, not as a finished product. You are the sculptor; you are the one with the power in your hands. If the piece of work is not as you would like, begin to recreate it.

Try tapping into your inner child, everyone has one. Enjoy the moments you spend there. Remember how it felt when life beckoned you, when anything seemed possible. Everyone is born with the capacity to be a winner. We are born without knowing the externally imposed limits on our potential. It's only as we get older and experience the knockbacks of life that negative beliefs become ingrained. Tell yourself that all you have done is learn them; they can be unlearned. If you examine your life thus far and view it with a positive slant I am sure you'll come up with occasions when you've had small victories. Use them to instil in you the confidence to see that you can succeed. Don't be discouraged by setbacks. Don't be afraid to make changes or to take some positive first steps. If you fall down, just pick yourself up and continue moving forwards. I promise that you will never regret it.

> All of us have bad luck and good luck. The man who persists
> through the bad luck, who keeps right on going – he is
> the man who is there when the good luck comes
> and he is ready to receive it
> *Robert Collier*

When you finally reach your goal, whatever it may be, you won't remember any of the setbacks you suffered or the pain of rejection or any of the hardship. Your mind will be filled with the satisfaction of knowing that you achieved what you set out to do. You will know that all those negatives are a thing of the past and that a rosy future of success awaits you.

It may be that you are happy to go with the flow and see where life takes you and, if so, that's great but you probably won't achieve financial security that way and it certainly won't make you rich. It has been said that those who are satisfied with their lot achieve the greatest happiness in life and that too may be so but I have found it's difficult to achieve happiness when the stress of not being able to make ends meet starts to bite. How can anyone be happy when the threat of redundancy or repossession hangs over their head?

The time to sit back, appreciate what you've got and become more settled comes as you reach the steps at the top, when the burden of financial worries has been relieved and you have enough time and hard cash to start thinking about the possibility of helping others or simply enjoying the profits of your hard work.

If you ask most people what they wish for in life for themselves or their children the most common answer they give is, 'I just want to be happy'. Personally I think it is much wiser to seek contentment rather than happiness. Although we like to believe that money doesn't buy happiness most people secretly think that it will. I accept that money can't buy true love (but it can attract an awful lot of admirers and buy a lot of sex!), it doesn't protect you from illness (but can buy medical insurance for better healthcare should you need it), it won't make you thinner, sexier, younger or give you lasting peace. It's not the answer to all life's problems; there are plenty of fat, ill, desperately unhappy, lonely rich people in the world with no genuine friends. And, as the old Chinese

proverb goes, you can buy the best bed but get no sleep. No,
money certainly is not a cure-all but it is the icing on the cake;
not the be-all and end-all of life but having enough of it makes
life a lot more bearable. What money can do is buy away some
unhappiness. In the very least it allows us to be miserable in
comfort!

The pursuit of happiness can last a lifetime, it is such an
elusive thing and many may feel they never actually attain
their goal. But contentment is achievable; you can work hard
and find contentment, you can relieve many of the stresses of
life by reaching financial security. That's a worthy quest and
something concrete to aim for. Happiness comes and goes but
contentment lasts.

Convinced? Good. You have commitment, that's a solid
start. Now as long as you follow my steps that lie ahead using
that commitment and determination I am confident that you
will succeed. I have done it myself. I had no money. I worked
long and hard and now I have achieved. Work like there's no
tomorrow and all your efforts will pay off tenfold. Graft like
you've never grafted before and watch as the rewards begin to
flow.

So if you have the willpower and determination to succeed,
have made up your mind to stick at it and work hard, I will show
you all I know about making money and how to build wealth,
making it work for you. I will tuck you under my wing and guide
you until you reach your goal. As long as you're ready and
willing to learn and will apply yourself with maximum effort, I
am absolutely confident that together we will get there.

Remember:

- No one can motivate you. They can encourage, threaten or
  inspire, but only you have the power to act
- Don't be a wanna-be or, even worse, a could've been; do
  not follow the crowd

- Once you discover your purpose you will find the passion to get motivated
- True motivation cannot be bought. You don't need money to find it – it comes from within. Dig deep and find a desire so strong that you need to take action

---

To accomplish great things, we must not only act,
but also dream; not only plan but also believe.
Anatole France

STEP 4

KNOW YOUR GOAL

The greater danger for most of us is not that our aim is too high and we miss it, but that it is too low and we reach it.
Michelangelo

This is an important step because, if you don't know where you're going, you can't possibly hope to get there. It's like leaving home without a route planned when setting off on a journey; if you have no destination in mind, you'll spend hours driving around in circles and end up nowhere.

I think one of the first objectives in this step is to decide on what your goal represents in material terms. Your planned objective may be to have a four-bedroom house all paid for by the time you are 45 or to be able to afford to treat friends or family whenever you like, fancy holidays in the sun or that dream car or even yacht. Obviously you must be realistic and your goal has to be achievable. Ambitious goals, yes; unrealistic and impossible, no. It's a good idea to aim high but setting impossible targets is simply demoralizing.

For example, setting yourself a goal of becoming wealthy enough to take over the Microsoft empire within ten years is an unrealistic plan, i.e. it's never going to happen. However, if you're interested in computers and technology, then setting yourself a goal of becoming trained and starting your own software company within ten years is both realistic and achievable.

Be honest with yourself; take some time to consider your strengths and weaknesses, your interests and talents. If you aren't interested in acting, suffer from stage fright and have absolutely no artistic talent, then setting an objective of becoming an international movie star is not being true to yourself and dooms your plan to failure. The *X-Factor* auditions are full of deluded people with no talent.

A word of advice when deciding your goals; don't feel obliged to tell others about them. Often the opinions of others can be negative. There are people who put a damper on ideas for a whole host of different reasons, usually nothing to do with the idea being a rotten one and quite often it's because they are frustrated with their own stagnation. Some people fear failure so much that they prefer never to enter the game. If they are close to you they will fear your failure and the effect it may have on you. If they feel they have failed in life, then subconsciously they will want you to fail too – probably not in a malicious way but if your life mirrors theirs they feel safe in the knowledge that you are like them, will remain like them and therefore they won't lose you.

It's often the case that the status quo, however unsatis-factory, is familiar and safe and they don't want their boat rocked if there's the risk it may capsize with them in it. To get carried along with the tide is so comforting that most people will not dare to swim against it. By straying from the route mapped out for you perhaps by self-limitation or low expecta-tions from family, you will find you can make differences in your life that may be far-reaching.

> Two roads diverged in a wood, and I – I took the one less
> traveled by, and that has made all the difference.
> *Robert Frost*

Make up your mind to break free from other people's expectations of you. That's what I did. And take it from me, it's therapeutic! Whether your goal is to be rich or just to feel happier in life, you must break free from others' expectations. As long as you have been realistic and honest with yourself, then there's no need to gauge yourself by the opinions of others. Even family members can be negative if they feel threatened by your change in attitude or plan to better yourself. The old adage 'they've got ideas above their station' makes me cringe but there are people who still set store by it. And the fact is that most people would rather flop in front of the television than drag themselves up and do something positive to improve their lives.

I find one of the conversations that irritates me the most is when people say, 'I just wish I could win the lottery. That's what I need to happen,' and then they embark on a pointless narration of how they would spend their money and what they would do with their life. I find it so tiresome because firstly it's highly unlikely to happen (the odds are estimated at fourteen million to one against winning the big one) and, secondly, if they want a taste of the good life why don't they reach out and grab it? The answer again is laziness. They want the rewards but don't want to put in the hard work. Where's the fun in that?

Hopefully by this stage in the book you have committed to the fact that if you want to live in the lap of luxury you'll have to work your socks off to get there. You'll have to get up early in the morning, work all day and go to bed planning how hard you're going to work the next day. You'll have to make sacrifices, perhaps study, put in maximum effort and never take your eye off the ball. I also hope that you've come to appreciate the feeling that taking control of your life and your finances gives you. You may be no financially better off now than when you picked up this book but I am almost certain you feel better. Knowing that you are going to take action to improve your life is empowering. You are already 'better off' than your lazy friends!

In order to achieve your goal you have to make an initial outlay but it's OK, you don't have to trot off to the bank for a loan. This down-payment comes from sweat, focus, commitment and passion. Without it you have no chance of succeeding but the good news is that you have a never-ending supply of all four; it's all a matter of choice. Make up your mind to work your fingers to the bone, don't give up and you'll get to the top of the steps, I promise.

In the words of the great Muhammad Ali, 'What keeps me going is goals,' and I believe this to be instrumental in the man's success. As I mentioned earlier, all the successful people I have met throughout my career have known where they want to be and have planned how to get there.

So before you move on to Step 5 I want you to know in your own mind how rich you intend to become. If you don't have a target how can you possibly take aim? How will you know when you've achieved success or monitor how you're doing as you climb the steps?

The great thing about money is that it knows no boundaries or discriminations. It is out there for all of us to strive for and to achieve. It will come to us if we work hard no matter what our sex, race, religion, class or age. It is there for the taking no matter what our education or qualifications. Once we accept that we are worthy of wealth, then we won't undermine our attempts to achieve it. It really is simply a case of applying yourself.

It may be that you will feel you have achieved success once you have made enough money to stop worrying about not having enough. For some people that may mean simply having an emergency savings fund to fall back on if the need arises. If that is the case I will help you achieve your goal within the next few steps. Others may feel that success will only come once they are living on the interest of the capital they have amassed, or perhaps even the interest on the interest. Whatever your goal, keep it in mind and don't let anything distract you from it. And the most important thing of all is to enjoy the climb.

A person who aims at nothing is sure to hit it.
Anon

STEP 5

ESTABLISH WHERE YOU STAND

Facts do not cease to exist because they are ignored.
Aldous Huxley

Hopefully you have built enough motivation by now to want to get on with the job without further delay. But before you go full steam ahead we need to find out exactly where you are now. The first task of this step is to take full stock of your financial situation, however ugly it may be at the moment. Be brave, take a deep breath, and have an honest and comprehensive look at the real situation. Discover what you owe, how much you are owed, any assets you may have, basically your net worth.

A full financial audit may reveal that your net worth is a negative figure, but please don't worry. Once we have established exactly where you stand we will pull out all the stops to turn the situation around. This time next year, provided you've followed my advice, I guarantee the same exercise will show a much improved picture. But for now, grit your teeth and let's get on with it; a wise man always lays out his tools before he begins the job.

Firstly, contact your mortgage provider and get an exact

figure for the sum outstanding on your mortgage. List the balances from your current account and deposit and savings accounts (if you have any) and what you owe on your credit cards and any outstanding loans. Table 1 is just a guide but may help you to organize the figures so that it's easier for you to see the full picture.

Table 1: Your financial position

Detail	Amount in credit	Amount owed	Net position
Bank current account	£	XXXXXX	
Savings accounts	£	XXXXXX	
Investments	£	XXXXXX	
Other savings	£	XXXXXX	
Mortgage	XXXXXX	£	
Loans	XXXXXX	£	
Credit cards	XXXXXX	£	
Other debts	XXXXXX	£	
Totals	£	£	

You then need to summarize your flow of moneys both in and out on a monthly basis. Before you do this, think of all the expenses you have on a quarterly or yearly basis and enter them onto a chart so that you can calculate a monthly figure. This is a worthwhile exercise in itself as it allows you to make monthly savings from this moment on so that expenses such as car insurance or car tax can be saved for in advance. It's almost always more economical to pay these in one lump sum (another example of the poor being poorer due to poor planning). Again, Table 2 may not suit your situation exactly but you can adapt it to your own needs and circumstances.

Establish Where You Stand

Table 2: Your annual expenses

Item	Yearly/ Quarterly fee	Monthly equivalent	Notes
Home insurance	£	£	
Car insurance	£	£	
Car tax	£	£	
MOT/Service	£	£	
Gas	£	£	
Electricity	£	£	
Water Rates	£	£	
Other	£	£	
Totals	£	£ **(A)**	

Table 3: Your monthly expenses

Item	Monthly expenditure	Notes
Mortgage/rent	£	
Petrol	£	
Food	£	
Council tax	£	
Gas	£	
Electricity	£	
Telephone	£	
Mobile phone	£	
Insurance	£	
Other	£	
Total	£ **(B)**	

Great, now we can move ahead with a summary of your expenditure, as illustrated by Table 3.

Add the total of A+B so you can clearly see your outgoings every month.

Now is not the time to start worrying. You are already looking down the correct path just by knowing where you stand; being an ostrich is no longer for you and certainly is not in my plans for your success!

Good. Let's take a look at your incoming money from all sources, as per Table 4.

Table 4: Your monthly income

Source of income	Amount per month	Notes
Main job	£	
Part-time job	£	
Working tax credit	£	
Child benefit	£	
Total	£ **(C)**	

This is where it heats up and you need to be brave. Take away the total of A and B from your income total of C. If you have surplus money, that's good. If you are just breaking even or are in a position of minus, don't panic!

It is important to record everything you can think of so have another look over the figures and remember not to worry if the situation appears none too rosy at the moment. Bearing in mind we have already established that setting goals is an excellent motivational tool we will now set a plan for moving you from the red into the black.

Don't forget that I have been where you are now; I look

back over my shoulder and see myself with an empty bank account. Now all that's there is a shadow veiled by my accomplishments. So please don't be distressed over the place you stand at the moment. I will help you rise above the murky depths of unmanageable finances. These things will change as soon as you face reality and begin to take action. I am here to help you turn your finances around.

STEP 6

MAKE A PLAN

To work well is to live well.
Thomas Aquinas, 13th century theologian

At this point I hope that you believe you can become wealthy and feel motivated enough to achieve your goals. Hopefully you now have a clear picture of where you are and where you want to be. The next step is to plan how you're going to get there.

There are no right or wrong answers in this step; the decision of how you aim to become wealthy has to be based on your personal likes and dislikes, talents and interests. Decide where your dreams lie. If you want to achieve your goal of prosperity you've got to be driven and this will be difficult to achieve if you've chosen a path that you feel lacklustre about. The author Gerald Durrell had a childhood dream of owning a zoo and he wrote 36 books, later to become bestsellers, in a massive effort and drive to achieve his dream (Jersey Zoo). He had an obvious talent for writing and exploited his talent to achieve his goal.

If, as mentioned in Step 4, your goal is to have a four-bedroom house, all paid for by the time you are 45, your plan should include the milestones you need to pass along the way, such as purchasing a studio flat within the next year, moving up to a two-bedroom flat within the next four years and so on until you reach your goal. As I said earlier, the successful people I know have all had a plan; they knew when and where and how.

'How' may seem the most difficult part of your plan. One thing to consider is whether you will achieve your goal by working for someone else or whether to go it alone. It is worth bearing in mind that there is always a limit to how much someone is willing to pay you in return for your labour. When working for yourself these constraints are removed. However, you will often be under far more pressure to perform, both with time and ability.

While it is true that entrepreneurs often enjoy greater prosperity, it is possible to carve for yourself a niche working for someone else and command a very decent salary. If you do this and plug all possible financial leaks you will still achieve wealth, provided you are willing to spend your time-off concentrating on another sideline, perhaps aiming for a buy-to-let property or establishing a portfolio of stocks and shares (see later steps).

A large number of my own clients have achieved financial security while being employed by investing wisely and taking good advice. If you enjoy stability and don't think you would enjoy the extra stress of being responsible for ensuring your own income and possibly others who work for you, then perhaps employment is the right path for you. The most important thing is to think about what would work best for you. Work should be satisfying and enjoyable. As I stress throughout the steps, you must make sure you enjoy what you do. If going to work is satisfying, you are far more likely to succeed.

If you decide to go it alone, it is wise to bear in mind that nearly two-thirds of new businesses end in failure within the first three years. I'm not saying that to put you off; on the contrary, I think working for yourself can sometimes pay great dividends. However, self-employment should never be seen as the easy option. It is vital to check the lie of the land, investigate the possibilities and make sure it's the right business for you. It sounds like a ridiculous example but opening a hairdressing salon in a town full of bald men is not going to propel anyone into mega-wealth. It's going to be over before it's begun. Do your market research and find out what demand there is out there for your services.

Your chances of being a winner are far higher if you can find a unique selling point, an unusual service or perhaps a mainstream service with a quirky approach. If you decide to go into a business that's already well established in the market (for example, launching your own cola brand) it has to have something very different about it, something unique that sets it apart from all the rest. Be innovative. If you carve yourself a niche market you can call the shots and command a premium income.

Remember to remain open-minded and flexible in your plan if you can. Life has a way of running off-course sometimes and with, 'the best laid plans of mice and men . . .' things don't always pan out as you might hope. Move skilfully and swiftly. If your idea for a business doesn't raise any interest in others you could maybe think of a different slant or change tack altogether. On the whole, growing industries or those that appear to be up and coming offer the greatest benefits, particularly if the start-up costs are fairly low. Never enter a swamped market.

Make sure you know the market very well or if you don't you must find out everything you can about it *before* you commit either yourself or one penny of capital. We're all more likely to be successful if we stick to what we know. If I, for example, were to try and write a novel I have little doubt that I would be laughed out of my editor's office pretty swiftly, with the manuscript I'd be likely to produce in tow. However, I settled on an area where I have expertise and therefore elicited a positive response.

It's also a good idea to care about what you do or at least have an interest in it. It's likely you'll be working in the new arena you choose for yourself for a long time and it's not all about building wealth. As I keep on emphasizing, you must enjoy the climb, or the years that follow will be wasted (in my opinion at least, though some of you may disagree).

Research your market and find out how to advertise yourself. No one's going to beat a path to your door offering you business. You have to be hungry for it. Go out and hunt for it, sniff out all the possibilities, create breaks wherever and whenever you can. Learning to sell is a vital tool in ensuring success. Whatever business you go into, you will have to sell a commodity, service, skills or ideas and it will also involve selling yourself (no, I don't mean in that way!). We'll learn more about the importance of sales technique in Step 17. For now, try to promote yourself without hesitation or reluctance because you can't make money without selling. If you can organize your business so that something is selling even while you're having a day off, or better still, while you're asleep, so much the better! Seize every opportunity to get the word out and then name your price.

Whichever path you choose, income from your day job is not the only path to prosperity. You should stay open-minded and get a finger in as many pies as possible. You can't go far wrong if you diversify. Richard Branson is a master of diversity; he has a finger in a shed load of pies and he's probably still dreaming up new ones. He has a proverbial egg in innumerable baskets.

There are a number of opportunities you can take advantage of if your choice is to remain in full-time employment (see Step 14). The door is open to everyone! Make a plan and cross the threshold to change your destiny as I changed mine.

Prepare your mind to receive the best that life has to offer.
Ernest Holmes

STEP 7

FOLLOW THE YELLOW BRICK ROAD

It is the brain, the little grey cells on which one must rely.
One must seek the truth within, not without.
Hercule Poirot

Agatha Christie's *Poirot* is a favourite of mine. I think it's because I feel an affinity with the man. For a start he loves the finer things in life – fine dining, very comfortable hotel rooms, excellent food – and he doesn't shy away from speaking his mind. He has a bit of an ego and firmly believes he is number 1 in his profession! But apart from being kindred spirits I admire his philosophy on life and his belief that the greatest tool he has is 'the psychology' and the 'little grey cells'. And, much to the bewilderment of his associate Captain Hastings, he solves many of his cases by thinking rather than dashing around chasing clues like some of the inferior detectives in crime novels.

I believe many hurdles in life can be overcome by a positive mental attitude and many races won by 'thinking' yourself over the finish line. It is now time for you to harness the positive attitude you are developing and use your 'little grey cells' to think yourself rich. I want you to take what you have learnt so far in your climb one step further by thinking yourself at the summit of our golden staircase.

So far in your climb you have accepted that it's never too late. You have hopefully overcome any negative feelings that may have held you back and worked up the motivation to make changes in your life. You know exactly where you are, where you want to be and have even cooked up a 'cunning plan' to get there. Now this step is easy; you just have to sit, ponder and watch it all happen.

So close your eyes. Imagine you are where you want to be. Whatever route you've chosen to reach your own personal pot of gold, feel yourself stepping out towards your destiny. See the golden path beneath your feet, feel the warm glow of success on your back, smell the fine wine beckoning you further, luring you closer to your goal. Sense the achievement, personal fulfilment and all the pleasures that your new-found wealth will bring.

> Test: Close your eyes. Imagine you are cutting into a lemon. Concentrate on the sight and smell of the fruit as you raise it to your lips, then imagine biting into it and sucking hard. Your taste buds will respond accordingly . . .

Concentrating on these rewards will bring them closer to you until they are within your grasp. Seeing is believing. Visualization techniques have been used for thousands of years to promote emotional and physical healing. Conjuring positive pictures in your mind really can alter emotions and have a marked effect on both your mind and body. They work.

I can personally vouch for that. I have often used concentration training and positive thinking techniques and still find them to be of enormous assistance to me, particularly when undertaking my TV work; answering viewers' questions can be very demanding! Try for yourself, as there are many distractions in life and the mind has a way of flitting randomly between them so that focusing on one thing can be a challenge.

Learning to focus the mind on an essential task is a discipline that can help you to excel in your endeavours. Switching off from negative thoughts or situations is of great benefit to anyone who is seeking success, either in academic terms, in business or even on the sports field. I am not one of those people who subscribe to the notion that winning isn't important and that it's the taking part that counts. Utter rubbish. Winning is everything. One-upmanship is the name of the game. If you don't aim to win, you're not showing respect to your opponents, not valuing the competition. And I've always been in it to win it. Having said that, being able to deal with failure positively is important, as Kipling put it, 'If you can meet with triumph and disaster and treat those two impostors just the same . . . yours is the earth and everything that's in it'.

Mental rehearsal has enabled me to 'win' in a number of situations when the odds were stacked against me. For example, a few years back I had booked a meeting with the board of a large UK company. This meeting was pivotal in clinching a very lucrative deal for Best Advice. I knew this was a window of opportunity that would not open for me twice. On the evening prior to the meeting I got the dreaded body aches, shivers and high temperature; in other words, severe man flu. In this state it was obvious I wouldn't be able to leave my bed in the morning, let alone take control of the meeting. Unable to think of anything else that would help, I visualized myself waking the following morning feeling great, no man flu, no aching body. I went through the whole morning in my mind, the meeting, the positive reception I hoped for, the successful outcome, I even imagined the restaurant I would take everyone to so that we could celebrate securing the deal. I'm not exaggerating when I tell you, my sceptical protégé, that I woke the next morning in perfect health. Needless to say, the meeting went as planned (as imagined anyway) and the deal was cemented by lunching very well indeed!

I think it helps to focus on the goal you need to achieve and, if necessary, break it into small manageable steps. By doing this you will gradually build confidence as each step is attained. For example, you may be working as a hairdresser in a local salon and your goal may be to have a salon of your own. You could set your first goal as investigating the costs associated with self trading. The next step could be exploring all the possible ways to advertise yourself once you go it alone. Once you've built up a regular clientele (maybe by doing mobile work after work) you will feel confident enough to make enquires about premises. It may seem too overwhelming (and not very sensible!) to quit your job and go into business employing others in one big step. It's often possible to break an overwhelming challenge into a series of small steps and then conquer each one individually. Visualize each stage and 'see' yourself moving confidently towards the next. This builds self-image and enough confidence to break out of your comfort zone.

Start by:

- Identifying a goal
- Visualizing rewards
- Keep thinking of your goal every day and see it clearly
- Focus on positive feelings
- Harnessing desire for personal satisfaction and use it to fuel motivation

- Visualize a successful outcome
- If you have a friend or associate who exudes positive energy tell him or her about your goal to boost encouragement

I want you to understand that I am a practical person. I'm not into the airy fairy side of life in which I include horoscopes, fortune telling, and crystal healing or attuning to the universe to be rewarded with your wishes in life; you need to work hard to get the support of the universe by being positive and resolute! I believe in hard work. But I want you to try this technique because it really does work and work well. Don't forget we all make our own luck. Good fortune comes to those who have foreseen it. You may even be using the technique already, subconsciously.

Many worriers automatically do it all the time without realizing it. They worry and fret about a future event/occurrence, and see all sorts of things going wrong. This is a negative use of visualization but they are halfway there. All they need to do is simply turn it on its head from 'glass half-empty' to 'glass half-full'; rather than visualizing all the things that will go wrong, begin to twist the kaleidoscope and see everything falling into place instead. If, in your 'mind's eye', all that you could possibly hope for actually happens, it is most likely that these things WILL come to be.

If you suffer from shyness and feel it holds you back from taking charge of business situations, the technique can be particularly helpful. Trina, my sister finds this in the course of her work. It is sometimes necessary for her to give presentations to large groups of people. She is not one of life's natural extroverts and finds this particular task a source of great anxiety.

I first explained the technique to her a few years ago and she tells me that it has been of great benefit to her ever since. On the evening prior to a presentation she visualizes everything, step by step; where she will stand, how she will introduce herself, every detail and each time it goes fabulously well in her head. She imagines the audience immediately warming to her and feels calm and in control. Familiarizing herself with future challenges is integral to her success. Each presentation now passes smoothly and her confidence has strengthened to the point where she sometimes forgets to use the technique because she is so unphased by these situations.

Visualization techniques are often used by top sportspeople as they assist in providing that competitive edge. A friend of mine is a rugby coach for under 16s and first started using the technique a few years back when the team his son was part of reached the final of a notable competition. They were unfortunate enough to come up against a team they had played many times before but never beaten. This chap gathered the kids around him before the match and asked them to think of all the things that could go wrong during play – dropped balls, missed tackles, knock ons, injuries, etc – and he asked them to imagine writing each one down on a piece of paper. They then had to imagine screwing the paper up into a tiny ball and throwing it away.

He then told them to think of all the good things that they wanted to happen in the match – making tackles, taking chances when presented, passes going to hand and catching, making breaks and winning turnovers. They went onto the pitch with these things foremost in their mind. To their delight they won the match and carried away the trophy!

I hope you now appreciate the value of mental rehearsal; it is a useful psychological trick that allows you to think of the thing you would most *like* to happen and transform it into reality. I find I gain great energy from imagery, it really psyches me up. It's mentally energizing. As a child I would lie awake seeing positive images of what and where I wanted to be; it was so clear I could even dream in colour! Much to everyone's amusement I called this 'Dargin'.

Remember to congratulate yourself on small victories and even if things go wrong praise yourself for making efforts and for completing the task. Move away from punishing yourself with negative thoughts. Get excited by the goals you set for yourself and use them to inspire positive thoughts by being:

- Passionate
- Enthusiastic
- Single minded
- Focused
- Determined
- Positive

So if it's a brand new sports car that motivates you I want you to throw on your mental blinkers, picture yourself gripping the leather steering wheel and taking corners at rip-roaring speed with the wind in your hair. Conjure visions of opulence and abundance and, I promise you, these things will be yours.

Imagine the scene, whatever it is that gets you going. Imagine how you would feel and then 'step' into that feeling. Visualize yourself on your own personal yellow brick road.

Points to remember about positive imagery:

- If you can harness the power of the mind your success can be unlimited
- It gets easier with practice
- Seeing it happen can make it happen

I believe I have said enough about the power of the mind and the benefits of positive thinking. You now stand on the landing above the first flight of steps. Hopefully you have the strength and motivation to move upwards on the second part of your climb towards riches. You have the willpower to make changes. Now I will take you through some practical changes that will lead to wealth. Follow me on my steps! All you have to do is stay the course.

PART TWO

STEPPING OUT TO MAKE CHANGES

STEP 8

KNOW YOUR MONEY

The more you know, the more luck you'll have.
Old Chinese proverb

Knowledge is power. Power overcomes fear. Fear strangles entrepreneurial spirit. By gaining knowledge you harness the power to move further towards your goal. You will get rid of your shackles and become free to pursue your dreams. Learn about money and you purge all negative preconceptions born out of ignorance.

Self-made millionaires usually make it their business to find out about money. Not only do they develop an understanding of money but they explore the principles of investing and saving. They show an interest in all aspects of money-making. They opt for the *Financial Times* rather than the frivolous sensationalist rags. They have a drive to learn about the thing they're chasing.

We all have little choice but to handle and manage money most days of our lives. Most of us have bank accounts and mortgages or rent-books, loans, overdrafts and credit cards. There is no hiding from it. We have no choice but to operate this way, so why not turn it to our advantage? Why not begin to understand it and take control by making money a friend and not our enemy? We have no need to be frightened of money or our lack of it. If we understand how to control our finances we can begin to enjoy our dealings with it.

And money is as fascinating to learn about as it is pleasurable to own. Did you know, for example, that the dollar is not made of paper at all? It is made from a special blend of cotton and linen and it is, in fact, slightly magnetic; there is metal in the ink.

Money itself is practically worthless of course. It's what money represents that gives it its value. Nothing demonstrates this fact quite as graphically as the tale of the old miser who buries his treasure of gold coins in the forest for safekeeping. Typical of an old scrooge he returns to the burial site every day, digs up his loot and counts it before hiding it away again. Unfortunately for him someone has been hiding behind the trees, watching his every move. The thief creeps into the forest under the cover of darkness and steals the entire fortune. The miser is devastated when he returns the next day to discover he has lost everything. When telling his friend of his woes he is told, 'Take a pile of stones and bury them in the hole. Make believe they are gold, for when the real treasure was there you made not the slightest use of it.'

What this story demonstrates is that notes and coins in themselves are of little worth; their value is symbolic. In fact, in our era of credit and debit cards it is possible to go from one year to the next without laying hands on any 'real' cash.

Until the seventh or eighth century, business was conducted without 'real' cash, and instead by way of a system of barter involving the exchange of goods, such as cattle, other livestock or grain. (Interestingly, the term 'capital', that is used to describe a lump sum of money, comes from the Latin word *caput* meaning movable property.) Often the exchange was not a fair one but necessity drove the 'sale'. For example, if a herdsman required the services of a carpenter he could perhaps exchange some milk or meat with the craftsman. Business relied on the fact that a carpenter needed these products. However milk and meat often did not accurately reflect the work the carpenter put into the project. If cattle were exchanged, further problems were caused since some were well-fed and others scrawny. Some might be in poor health or elderly and they required upkeep once ownership accepted. It was difficult to find a standard to measure fairly the true worth of goods or services exchanged.

In an effort to make trade fairer a medium of exchange that could be split, measured and negotiated was introduced. A portable 'object' that could be counted out was considered a viable option and then tradesmen would see clearly exactly where they stood. It is believed that writing was developed out of a need for keeping a tally of accounts.

Many items have been used as currency throughout the ages, from shells to glass (Manhattan Island was bartered for twenty four dollars' worth of glass trinkets). One of the earliest representations of money was tanned hides, useful because they were not perishable like grain or meat. Money made from leather was used in Russia (still used until the seventeenth century) and tea money was exchanged in China. Gold dust was legal tender during the Alaska Gold Rush. Other forms of legal tender have included gunpowder, pig's skulls, slaves and glass beads. If you had a number of skulls in Borneo you would have been considered well-off. In the early 1930s in Washington, USA, notes were temporarily made of wood during a crisis of cash shortage.

Money made from iron was used in ancient Sparta and it is said that the Spartan monarchs made the coins so large that its citizens never summoned the strength to leave the country with their wealth.

Gradually, coins of a uniform size and weight were manufactured and then stamped with their value. Basically the early coins were very like what remain today, a piece of metal whose worth has been guaranteed. Early evidence shows that coins made of silver existed in Iran in 650 BC. Also around this time metal coins were minted in Lydia, a kingdom in Asia Minor. When coins were made of precious metal, cunning thieves would shave off tiny pieces and save them up until they had enough to melt into bullion.

With the arrival of the Roman Empire came a form of gold standard. Reserves of gold were stored in the Temple of Juno Moneta which later became the royal mint. Juno was considered the goddess of money. The coins, minted in the temple, could be seen melted in the floor of the ruins following a fire which led to its destruction.

Nowadays the movement of wealth is largely a simple movement of paper or electronic exchange. It is difficult to estimate the amount of money that exists in the world today, since the value of each currency (of which there are roughly 174) changes daily. There is an estimated $49.7 billion in gold bullion held in various banks around the world however, with the largest chunk $17 billion held in a vault in the Federal Reserve Bank of New York.

Now that you have some understanding of the origins of money I want to help manoeuvre you into a position where some of this wealth out there becomes yours. I want you to have a piece of the action. Now that you have good knowledge of money you are sufficiently armed to move on to the next step where you pass on what you've learnt to the next generation.

And so I will close this step with some interesting and thought-provoking facts about the power of Money:

• Money is the leading cause of disagreements in marriage

- Most people fantasize more about money than sex . . . Wow!
- You are three times more likely to be killed in a car accident if you drive 10 miles to buy a lottery ticket than you are of winning the jackpot. (Best buy online . . . lol.)
- Many millionaires in the USA think of themselves as working class because they are often surrounded by people richer than they are

STEP 9

SAVE AS THEY GROW; TEACH THE NEXT GENERATION

One generation plants trees and the next enjoys the shade.
David Lloyd George, British Prime Minister (1863–1945)

Having demonstrated in Step 2 that it's never too late, I may appear a little contradictory when I say that it is important to teach children the importance of learning to save. To understand the value of money is an important lesson in life and the earlier we learn it, the less we will struggle with finances when we're older.

Teaching children the value of money will pay them great dividends in the long run and will save you an awful lot of money in the short term. I will show you a number of ways to enlist the help of your children in your climb to a richer future and they may just learn lessons in self-respect and the importance of generosity on the journey. Remember that poverty provides some valuable lessons too. Let them learn these while you're still poor because time will soon be running out!

In fact, I think there is no better start for children than a modest one. I grew up in inner London and we were poor. I'm not saying

I was raised in a slum, our house was always clean and tidy but we got by without luxuries. We had an outside toilet and no bath-room. On Sundays my Father would drag the old tin bath into the kitchen and Mother would start filling it with water boiled in saucepans. We all then took turns to have a bath (fortunately I was the eldest and so qualified for first go!). I won't go on but you get the picture. Money was tight and there was little left over for treats. Did I mind? Not a bit. Not having an indoor bathroom meant fewer baths and more time for play. We had a back yard and I had my brother and sister to terrorize, that was enough for me. Material things matter to adults far more than children.

I think that my humble beginnings allow me to appreciate so much more the things I have achieved and the luxuries I can afford now. I believe that it is wise to limit the material world in your children's lives if you achieve great wealth while they're still young. You will be doing them a favour. Let them spend their day in scruffs, tumbling in mud and splashing in puddles. Designer gear will detract from their fun, not improve their quality of life.

Teaching them to 'get by without' is a lesson that will serve them well throughout their life. Don't mollycoddle them with handouts for every little thing their heart desires. That's the biggest humdinger you can make as a wealthy parent. They'll never learn to respect or value money. They'll never learn to save. If children get into the mindset of saving from an early age it comes naturally to them. A good way of encouraging them is to give them an allowance each month and encourage them to put half away for savings. The rest they can spend as they choose but don't bail them out at the end of the month and they'll soon learn to budget. A friend of mine gives her children their allowance and they spend half, put one quarter in a savings account to save for big treats and one quarter in an account for their university years.

Another benefit of teaching children the principles of

money management and the value of money is that hopefully they will avoid slipping into the easy credit trap. To learn early that, if they want something they have to save for it, is such a valuable lesson and soon becomes second nature.

The Government has now recognized that teaching the young how to manage money should be a priority as a result of the tidal wave of debt spiralling out of control. Credit card and personal debt has now exceeded 1 trillion pounds in the UK alone. I believe money management will enter the school curriculum in the very near future in an attempt to stem the tide. This is vital if the future of the UK economy is to be secured.

A good introduction to the subject of money management is to have an initial chat with them to find out what they think and what they know about money. You may find that you get some amusing and random replies, especially from really young children. They may have heard it said that money doesn't grow on trees, however most children have no idea where money comes from. Explaining in more detail the origin of money can help them gain a good understanding. As soon as they can understand that money is earned by working and to spend all that you earn is foolish, the more secure their future will be.

Start to talk about money; how it's earned, where it's made, etc. Children are naturally inquisitive and will generally respond well, especially if you let them think it's all a bit of a game; you don't have to sit them down and bombard them with economic facts. Teaching our children about our complex financial system seems a big task, however it is worth your time and effort to help your children learn about money and avoid future stress and possible financial ruin!

Aim to teach them to:

• Develop strong saving habits, the younger the better

• Make wise financial choices – the UK financial institutions have realized that the key to their future profits and success is to capture the young; we need to teach our children to be vigilant, in order to make an informed choice

- Buy smart – there are many excellent ways to save but big gaps between the worst and the very best

- Avoid debt. There's over £1 trillion already in the UK. Let's help the next generation to be free of this financial ball and chain

- Learn that there is not a magic machine in dad's pocket/mum's purse, ready to spout money when pressed hard enough . . .

There are a number of fun ways to teach children to enjoy planning and organizing their finances:

- When they are very young let them use Smarties to count. Teach them not to eat the whole tube but to place around 20 per cent of the sweets in a container for tomorrow. This is an excellent way of teaching the concept of living for today but saving for tomorrow. As the children grow older having the same strategy for their money is then far more easily accepted if this system is started from a young age

- Open a bank account in their name so that they can see their savings grow; there are many accounts to choose from these days

- Allow them to withdraw money from savings if they want something really special

- Use a piggy bank or even a jar to make saving fun. Use the piggy bank to explain how real banks 'look after' money

- Sit with them and discuss a monthly budget. They can try to raise it and you can have fun bartering. Every pound they negotiate out of you will be valued by them, but don't give in easily

- If they manage to save some money, reward them with a small additional amount explaining that this happens at work if you do well, by bonus or commission payments, just like a bank pays interest

- At the end of each month calculate how much they have saved and then how much they have gained by interest and the bonus you have paid to them

- Plot a visual chart of their savings (including their goal and what it means for them) so they can easily see their savings grow. Keep it simple, geared to your own child's level of understanding

- Let them scrimp and save on the allowance and make it last to the end of the month. Subbing them is a cardinal sin – DON'T do it; all your good teaching will be blown in less time than it takes to reach into your purse . . .

Besides teaching them how to manage money you can use the opportunity and exploit it by managing their behaviour as a by-product by following my scheme 'Positive Play Time' known as PPT . . . Of course let them know that you intend to start a rewards system with points representing pennies and pounds. Positive behaviour earns them points and negative behaviour results in points being deducted. You will find they spend more time 'earning' privileges and less time being naughty. Table 5 is a guide to how PPT works:

Table 5: Positive Play Time (PPT)

Event	Week 1	Week 2	Week 3	Week 4
Tidied room	5	10	10	10
Laid the table	10	10	10	10
Being good	5	5	10	10
Cleaned the car	5	5	5	5
Bonus tokens	5	5	5	5
Tokens earned	*30*	*35*	*40*	*40*
Less negative tokens	10 (explain reasons)	8 (explain reasons)	7 (explain reasons)	0 (explain reasons)
Net earned	*20*	*27*	*33*	*40*
Rewards				
Visit cinema (20 tokens)				
Favourite restaurant (15 tokens)	15			
Hire DVD (10 tokens) Sub-total to c/f	5			

Not only does my system get them to think about their behaviour and its consequences, it also teaches them to think in the long term. They will begin to understand the concept of saving for tomorrow and the benefits of making efforts to get rewards.

Alongside the chart you would display a graph or bar chart such as the one overleaf:

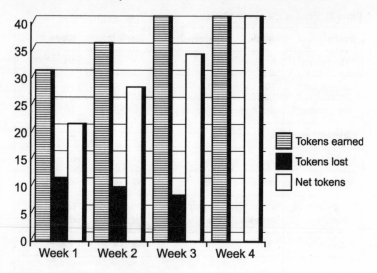

Fig. 1: Graph of token activity

This gives children a visual guide to how well they're doing over a period of weeks or months. They will see their own progress which is an excellent positive reinforcement and a further aid to learning about finance.

I am currently proposing this system to the Department for Children, Schools and Families to encourage knowledge of finance which is currently dire and to help behaviour issues which are even worse! Visit www.paulbanfield.co.uk for the full game details.

Now that you have them hooked, you can get them excited about saving as well by telling them they'll get freebies when they open a bank account. There is no limit to the number of accounts they're allowed to open so why not open a few different accounts? They'll love that! Minimum deposit is usually just £1 and they can think of different purposes for each account. For example, one account could be used to save for holiday spending money, one for university, one for electronic games, etc. Remember to shop around for the best rates since they vary substantially. For savings accounts available currently on the market for children the difference in interest between the best and the worst if investing £1,500 as a lump sum would be around £40 per year. That's too much to lose if you inadvertently have chosen the lowest account. Involve them in searching for the best deals so they get an idea of how to compare rates.

The following is a guide but remember rates change regularly:

- NS&I – Children's Bonus Bonds 3.7 per cent compound for 5 years – tax free – minimum £25, maximum £3,000

There are a number of regular savings accounts for children that pay high interest rates even with small balances:

- Halifax currently pays 10 per cent per annum fixed for one year, on savings of £10 to £100 per month

As you can see, the savings rates are far higher than those available for adults, even those with significant wealth, and this is often the case as the banks clamber to 'catch them' while young. If children have a bank book or statement, they can see the positive benefits of savings and it's fun for them to see the balance grow each month. Once they reach the age of 11 they can generally use their own ATM card (this is a further incentive for them). They feel grown up and it can encourage them to take responsibility; Halifax allows children to hold a VISA electron card from the age of 11 and allows withdrawals of up to £300 a day from cash machines and allows for purchases at retailers accepting VISA electron. Barclays, HSBC and Abbey offer a similar account and card facility from the same age, as do most high street banks and building societies. From the age of 13 HSBC offers a 'Solo' card allowing for purchases in shops.

There are tax advantages when you invest in a child's name (see also Step 20) so it is a good idea all round to encourage children to catch the savings bug. When I say there are tax advantages I don't mean that children's savings are exempt from tax or are tax-free. This is a common misconception; technically they're not. Children have an annual personal allowance of £6,035 (tax year 2008/09) as do adults, but since children don't use their allowance up with earnings it usually means their savings are safe from the taxman.

It's also a good idea to get grandparents involved in the idea of saving for their grandchildren. If the trustee of their account is a grandparent, the child's full personal tax allowance is available to them. If the parents are trustees, then only the first £100 in interest is tax free. Not only is it a wise move in respect of your children's future but it may help to avoid unwanted and inappropriate presents; grandparents will be encouraged to deposit money in the account as a present rather than buying gifts that sometimes are little used. This is especially beneficial as your children get older and are less interested in plastic toys.

In fact, children can now have a pension for their birthday box! Yes I jest not! It's true. It could be the greatest gift they'll ever receive. Some parents or grandparents now start pension provision for their children at birth. Using the new stakeholder pension legislation anyone can pay up to £3,600 per annum into a pension without proof of earnings.

Take a look at the following chart. It shows the value of a pension pot at retirement if contributions are made from birth until 60:

Monthly contribution from age 0 until age 60, after we've added in tax relief so the cost is only £80	£100

Now let's see what this would be worth at age 60 if the fund had 7 per cent growth per year . . .

Projected fund value at age 60	£692,000
Monthly income at selected retirement age 60	£3,325
Or a tax-free lump sum of	£173,000
And a reduced monthly income at selected retirement age 60	£2,416

Now compare this with the results from the chart below with a contribution of £100 gross per month from age 18 to age 60. See how much lower the projections are for the same contribution each month but starting at age 18 instead of at birth.

It pays so much to start at a young age!

| Monthly contribution from age 18 until age 60, after we've added in tax relief so the cost is only £80 | £100 |

Projected fund value at age 60	£223,000
Monthly income at selected retirement age 60	£1,075
Or a tax-free lump sum of	£55,800
And a reduced monthly income at selected retirement age 60	£810

So you can see that by maximizing the pension contributions from age 0 to 18 the total pension pot increases over 300 per cent.

Are you now convinced of the importance of getting the little people to save? Can you appreciate the benefits of saving on their behalf as soon as you are in a position to do so?

Let's move on to the Child Trust Fund, which is a long-term savings and investment account where your child (and no one else) can withdraw the money when they turn 18. There are a number of benefits of starting a fund for your child including:

- Neither you nor your child will pay tax on income and gains in the account
- £250 voucher to start each child's account from the Government
- Children in families receiving Child Tax Credit (CTC), with a household income not greater than the CTC threshold of £15,575 for 2008/09 will receive an extra payment

A maximum of £1,200 each year can be saved in the account by parents, family or friends but bear in mind that money cannot be taken out of the Child Trust Fund (CTF) once it has been put in. Your children can get their hands on the money once they reach the age of 18, although they can start to make decisions about how the money is managed when they are 16.

A further contribution of £250 will be inserted into the fund by the Government when your child reaches the age of 7 and if you have a low income an additional £250 will be invested. The money gets paid direct into their account around the time of their birthday.

The reason the Government introduced the Child Trust Fund in the first place and why they're willing to make these contributions is due to spiralling debt that is so rife in the UK. By taking steps now to ensure that the young learn how to become financially competent they hope to reverse this 'buy now, pay later culture'. They hope that their efforts to encourage a saving mentality will:

- Ensure your child has savings at the age of 18
- Teach your child about the benefits of saving

- Help your child understand personal finance
- Help reduce future borrowing and the current free-and-easy credit culture

There are three types of account available and you can choose which one suits you best, depending on how you feel about taking a risk in order to give the money a better chance to grow. At any time you can move the account to a different provider or change the type of account. You can contribute up to £1,200 in any one year (this does not include contributions from the Government).

So which type of account might be best for your child? The accounts available are:

Straightforward savings account – This is a safe choice and will pay interest on the savings. It probably won't perform as well as if invested in shares over the long term especially when considering inflation.

Shares account – The money your child invests is used to buy shares in companies and has the potential to perform very well in the long term. Of course this is a riskier investment than a straightforward savings account as it is possible that the companies perform poorly but, as a general rule, the poor performance of shares in some years is made up for in other years and the stock market value over time tends to rise rather than fall. However, money invested this way has grown more than the same amount placed in a savings account for every 18 year period in the last 40 years.

Stakeholder account – The investment is not used to buy shares in just one company but in a number of different companies to reduce the risk and once your child reaches 13 the money is gradually moved to lower risk investments depending on how well the shares are performing. There are charges but they are limited to ensure they do not exceed 1.5 per cent each year.

The Children's Mutual is the largest supplier of CTFs (one in five) also Selftrade allows you actively to trade shares within a CTF on a child's behalf.

For more info on the Child Trust Fund check out: www.childtrustfund.gov.uk

If you wish to give your children money outside of the CTF and the income they receive provides over £100 interest or income per year it will be taxed as if it's your own income but there are some ways to invest money for them where this is not the case:

- **Savings accounts** – If a grandparent is the trustee, the child will not pay any tax up to his or her personal allowance

- **Friendly Societies** – These are mutual organizations where investors become members of the society. They offer tax-free savings for children, similar to the Child Trust Fund

- **National Savings** – Some National Savings products are specially designed for children and all capital is 100 per cent backed by the British Government. Check out www.nsandi.com

- **ISAs** – From the age of 16 your child can hold a tax-free Cash ISA (Individual Savings Account) in his or her own name

Remember that whichever path you choose to help them to save they'll be learning valuable lessons along the way, lessons that perhaps if you had learned earlier in life would have made a financial difference. A big bonus is that you can be safe in the knowledge that when you manage to acquire great wealth it will now be safe in the hands of your beneficiaries!

STEP 10

PLUG THOSE LEAKS

Once I was definitely on the firm ground, my brain began to work once more with its normal brilliance.
Hercule Poirot

The poor are penalized. That is an ugly fact, but usually the penalties can be avoided with foresight and good planning. A fool and his money are so easily parted because the fool doesn't work to a plan. By making a plan and sticking to it you can avoid the poverty trap. I'm not suggesting you mess around with small economies that will save you a few pennies but make you entirely miserable. Banning little everyday luxuries to save a few extra pounds won't make you wealthy but will make the climb all the steeper.

If your bag is to indulge yourself with a glass of good red wine at the end of a hectic day, please continue to do so. Adding an extra five pounds to the pot won't make you prosperous but will make you resentful and may begin to undermine your determination. One of my aims in writing this book is not only to help you to become rich but also to enhance your life as you climb. Little treats can make a bad day turn good. Denying small pleasures in life is satisfying for some people – they enjoy the discipline of being frugal – but it isn't necessary. Throwing money away by being careless is going to be an obstacle to wealth and this is where you should focus your attention.

Think of it as a diet. If you decide to lose weight and deny yourself anything and everything you enjoy, your diet will be doomed to failure. Allowing little treats along the way doesn't upset your mindset and encourages you to continue along the same path. On the other hand, I'm not suggesting you go mad and buy everything you wish for! This will also doom our plans to failure. Strike a balance. Buy less, buy good quality and never ever use credit. If you want to make a big purchase, then save for it. It can be difficult to resist the temptation to 'buy now, pay later', particularly when the most tempting offers of easy finance land regularly on your doormat, but try to be strong and get in the mindset of the rich. Wealthy people don't scrimp and save every last penny but they do plug the leaks, they watch over their money and don't give it away unnecessarily.

This step helps you to follow the rules of the rich, plugs in all the holes, making sure that your money is not leaking away. So many people sit back and let it happen, afraid of taking an honest look at their finances and reluctant to put in the effort to correct bad or lazy practices. If you have debts, then your top priority must be to clear these first. It is absolutely pointless embarking on any money-making schemes or investments when debts are swallowing up your cash like there's no tomorrow.

If you have debts but also have money in savings, your first priority should be to clear some of the debt with your savings. It is pointless earning 4 per cent or 5 per cent on savings only to be paying anything from 7+ per cent in interest payments. Offset savings against loans and reduce the total amount of interest you pay. Borrowers pay a higher rate of interest than savers receive (otherwise we'd all be borrowing a fortune and investing it in high interest amounts to make a killing!).

There may be the odd exception where it pays to borrow money to make an investment elsewhere (you will always need professional advice here) but this is more of a risk than investing money that is yours to start with. It is far wiser to clear the debts if you have any and only play with money when you can truly afford to. Work, work and yet more work is the key to financial freedom. Borrowing to finance the start-up costs of a business is slightly different and not necessarily a bad idea, but only borrow if you absolutely have no other choice and then you must do your research and choose the loan wisely.

If you are unable to save enough to clear your debts in the near future it is sometimes sensible to consolidate your loans to one monthly payment with an overall lower interest rate, even to start with extending the term of years if you find you are not meeting your current commitments. This will help you to manage and will bring with it the buzz from the feel-good factor! Obviously the most sensible thing is to avoid taking loans in the first place, but if you have them don't worry, you're certainly not alone. For the short term you're stuck with them and so the next best thing to do is to pay as little interest as possible and get them cleared as a matter of urgency.

A number of new clients who have requested my help and advice have been trapped in this woeful situation, often paying interest on a varying number of credit cards, all with chokingly high interest rates, plus juggling with large overdraft and loans. The credit bubble is in the process of bursting. Don't be caught up in the fall-out. Debts are a millstone around the neck. You can never be entirely care-free with the nagging worries about interest payments forever bogging you down. Debt prevents us from moving forwards and does little for our health. (I'm not classing mortgages as debts because although we pay interest on the borrowed monies it is an investment and so they are very different.)

Cut up all credit cards today, and shop around for one large loan to encompass all of your debts plus overdraft. Obviously go for the lowest interest rate but be careful not to get tied into a long-term loan. The best option is to go for one that will allow you to pay off chunks of the loan without penalizing you so that you can achieve your aim of clearing your debts at the earliest opportunity. This will help you to gain from the feel-good factor.

Top tips for loan consolidation:

- Choose a loan over the shortest term that you can afford – the shorter the term, the less interest you'll pay
- Go for a loan with no penalties for early clearance
- Only secure the loan against your home if you are absolutely confident that you have contingency plans to pay the loan if you encounter problems. (You will often secure a lower rate of interest for secured loans but is it worth the risk?)
- Don't go for the easy option and ask your bank manager for a loan – it's often not the best and it pays to shop around
- Make use of the internet to do the legwork for you
- Be wary of companies offering to consolidate your loans for you; check out the interest rate
- Do take advice. An independent financial adviser or the Citizens Advice Bureau will be able to help you
- READ THE SMALL PRINT!

If you are having difficulty paying your debts or you are behind with your payments, it is also worth contacting your creditors as soon as possible. They may agree to reduce your monthly payments or extend the term of the loan. This will help you in the short term and you can work towards reducing the debt without receiving a County Court Judgement (CCJ) for non payment which would reduce your credit rating and make it difficult when applying for, say, a mortgage in the future. It's certainly worth asking and they may accept your proposal as you have shown good faith. You can then, as your credit rating improves, raise one loan to clear all the debts. But make sure you can afford the monthly payments by selecting the term of the loan as required.

Tackling spending excesses is also essential, as I have mentioned before. Cut up your credit cards; it's no good keeping them 'just in case'. They have a seductive power that many find irresistible. Debts can be racked up into unmanageable amounts over the period of just a few months. If you want to be wealthy you must resist impulse buying for short-term satisfaction and focus on long-term goals only.

Keep a record of every penny you spend so you have an exact idea of where your cash is going and where your weaknesses lie. Always check your bank balance and ensure that each item is correct; banks do make mistakes and unless you check your account and balance it monthly you will never notice. The rich remain on the ball always and never miss a trick when it comes to their money. Often people who run on overdraft do not check their account balances because they cannot stand to look. Living in denial or turning a blind eye is not part of my plan for you. Be brave, I promise I will help you.

Suffering from a lack of money over a long period is very hard to cope with. Consider making the following common-sense changes to lifestyle that can make a real difference:

• Cut driving speed from 70mph to 60mph – this has the effect of cutting petrol costs by 15 per cent

- Swap 100W light-bulbs for 60W – this saves 40 per cent on operating costs
- Switch off electrical appliances when not in use – a television on stand-by mode uses one third the power as when switched on
- Take to work a packed lunch and drink – saving just £5 per working day will amount to a massive £1,300 each year
- Use the internet in your lunchtime, if allowed at work, to find the best prices for any purchases you have in mind – a few minutes surfing could save a small fortune
- Walking to work or even cycling saves pounds per day on travel costs and you feel better for it too
- Smokers: I know you've seen all the gruesome adverts on TV but, look, I am The Money GP, this is one habit that has to go!

Not only will these tips be healthy for your finances but you will be doing your bit for the environment as well.

Points to remember when plugging those leaks:

- If you can't afford it, don't buy it. Unless it's shelter or food or clothing *why do you need it?!*
- No more borrowing – go without!
- Save spare cash for a rainy day – work on the principle that one day you may be in dire need of the cash
- The desire for material things can be as powerful as lust – go take a cold shower. Now is the time for control

STEP 11

BEAT THE CREDIT CRUNCH

Money, it turned out, was exactly like sex. You thought of nothing else if you didn't have it, and thought of other things if you did.
James Baldwin

Sounds like a simple step, not rocket science at least. But you'd be amazed at the number of people who ignore, disregard or remain woefully oblivious of its meaning even while the UK is in the middle of an economic downturn. The simple truth is that, if you spend more than you earn, you'll be living on credit and the cycle of poverty will continue into your retirement and old age.

Credit over the past few years has been so easily available and so incredibly seductive. We have all been bombarded with offers of loans, whether we can afford to repay them or not. The key is to recognize the danger in accepting them, realizing the penalties in the long term. Borrowing may get you what you want in the short term but you'll pay back heavily with loan repayments and interest. Neither a borrower nor a lender be. This has nothing to do with morals; it's just common sense. Borrow money and you'll end up the loser, always. If someone lends you money, they want it back 'and then some'. Unless you are offered an interest-free, no strings loan (an unlikely event) then say 'no', without exception. Say 'no' to loans; just don't go there, ever.

Now I always prefer to see credit cards cut in half as you know, but if you are absolutely sure you will not be tempted to use and abuse I will show you the right way to work with that little square of plastic.

Before, a word of warning . . . If you abuse them you'll end up in the basement with little to show for your climb but enormous APR.

However, if used cleverly, credit cards can actually assist you on your route to wealth. This is possible because many credit card companies these days offer very attractive introductory deals such as an interest-free period on new purchases. Sometimes the interest-free period can be up to a year or even longer. If you make all your usual household expenses plus petrol and any other purchases, you can use the 'cash' you save either to pay off some of your mortgage or to save in a high interest savings account. Make sure you settle the minimum payment each month (can be up to 5 per cent of the outstanding balance) and then at the end of the interest-free term you can use the money you've saved to pay off the balance in full or apply for a card that accepts balance transfers at zero per cent. This way you minimize the total amount you are paying in interest and hang on to your money for the maximum time.

Remember it's a must to keep the money you're saving aside each month so that you have a lump sum to pay off the balance on your credit card when the zero per cent offer expires or you undo all the good work you've done. Remember: when the interest-free period expires, the interest rate usually soars to around 16 per cent or higher, so be aware!

So if you are good at managing money to some extent already, you don't necessarily need to cut up the evil credit cards, just be very clever how you use them. There are pitfalls to watch out for and I've summarized the main ones below:

- Don't withdraw cash using your credit card – you'll be charged for the privilege and the interest-free period doesn't extend to cash withdrawals

- Never leave balances sitting on cards once the interest-free period has expired – over the years the debt will pile up to unmanageable proportions

- Look out for low-use fees – some card companies charge you for not using your card so close down any accounts you don't intend to use regularly

- Make sure you know the APR on the card you apply for – they can soar to 30–40 per cent

- Don't leave any credit on your credit card – you may be charged for it. This can happen if you return goods and get a refund issued on your card – some blood-sucking companies will charge you a £10 fee!

- Never say yes to PPI, payment protection – better to save for a rainy day than be ripped off

- Don't ever make use of credit card cheques – card providers sometimes send them through the post to tempt you. Make sure you shred them before the postman reaches the end of your path

Generally the rule should be that if you want something you can't afford, then go without. There is nothing more motivating than the drive to achieve or own something. If you want it badly enough, then work your socks off to get it. Chances are that once you have enough money for it the novelty will have worn off anyway.

Right, so we've established that incorrect use of credit cards and loans sets the path to financial ruin, agreed? And in Step 10 we've dealt with important areas where money can 'leak' out of control and looked at plugging as many holes as we can think of. The next step is to follow some simple rules for economizing so that they become a way of life. It won't feel as if you're scrimping, we've already agreed that life is too short to live like a miser. It's simply a case of making use of sensible ideas that can help to establish financial stability.

If, after conducting the exercise in Step 5 you found that your expenditure is more than your income, you need to make some immediate cutbacks. One area that most people find they can cut down on is their weekly shopping bill. Writing a list before you go to the shop sounds like an obvious tip but many people don't do this and over buy as a result. (Never shop when hungry!) Don't forget vouchers and tokens either – make it a habit to collect these when you come across them and then remember to use them. You'll be amazed how much you can save – the wealthy do it! It's not a case of penny pinching; it just makes sense to cut unnecessary waste – nowadays some supermarkets even accept their competitors' vouchers and tokens.

Forget takeaways and meals out for the short-term future. As you reach the next couple of steps you can dine out as much as you like if it gives you pleasure, but for now the priority is to get your income and expenses balanced at the very least. Once you have an adequate source of income the treat of a meal out will be all the sweeter knowing that (a) you've waited a while for it, (b) you've worked damned hard for it and, best of all, (c) you can afford it!

I know it is a pain but play the Scrooge for a while, just until your next financial check-up looks a little rosier. Hang on to what you've got and don't let money slip through your fingers. Control yourself and look forward to the day when you can let go – if you follow my advice it won't be too far away. Tighten your belt and this time next year you'll be so pleased that you did. Curbing the urge to have it all now is what the rich are good at; you just have to play by the same game.

Many people spend an awful lot of money they can't afford on new clothes. Later on we discover the importance of being meticulously smart and I'm not contradicting myself here. It is possible to look smart at all times but not spend a fortune on clothing. Personal grooming costs very little except time. Take care of the clothes you have and make up your mind not to indulge in new purchases until you have the ready cash to pay for them. If you have lots of old clothes that aren't suitable for your new venture, then sell them at a boot sale and use the proceeds to buy a new or nearly new suit.

And the final but most golden rule of all is to think before you buy anything. Do you really NEED it? Put some space between you and temptation. Give yourself a week to think about it before buying. You will probably find that time has weakened your urge to buy and you'll be instantly better off.

If you decide you do need to buy an item, make good use of price comparison sites on the net. It's an excellent way of making money stretch a little further. I recommend the following:

www.kelkoo.co.uk
www.pricerunner.co.uk
www.easyValue.com
www.checkaprice.com
www.froogle.co.uk

Once you've identified the cheapest supplier for the goods, log onto one of the cashback sites to make the purchase. These sites negotiate a lower price with the supplier and then split the revenue they earn with you. It's possible to save as much as 35 per cent on many products compared to traditional shopping. Try:

www.Rpoints.co.uk
www.greasypalm.co.uk

Another way to save hundreds of pounds a year on purchases is to learn the art of haggling. I know it's considered to be 'not British' but, if you can learn the art of driving a hard bargain, you can save a fortune on most purchases. Try it on all sorts of items: clothing, jewellery, electronic gadgets and particularly the more expensive goods.

Trawl the price comparison sites mentioned above and then approach the retailer of your choice and tell them you've seen the product they're selling cheaper on the net. Most will choose to take your business, particularly when goods are sometimes marked up by 60 per cent or even 70 per cent. Go in with confidence, as this approach works best, and be friendly, keeping the conversation warm. If the sales staff are unwilling to haggle, ask to speak with the manager and, if he won't play ball, ask to speak to someone at head office.

Try securing a better deal when you come to the end of your mobile telephone contract; companies will often come up with a much better deal with extra free texts and minutes or a lower monthly fee if they believe you'll take your business elsewhere. Similarly, if your credit card contract is nearing the end of its special deal, make sure you ask for a lower APR for the following term. If they refuse, simply check the comparison sites and find someone else who offers what you're looking for.

Most people are accustomed to bargaining without

embarrassment when it comes to buying a car or a house and this is so widely known that most sellers are willing to drop at least 5 per cent on the asking price. If you aren't willing to negotiate, you'll end up paying way over the odds. You can even drive a bargain on the cost of a holiday these days – take a look at www.priceline.co.uk where you can make offers for rooms in 15,000 European hotels. If you're willing to take a break at short notice, you can save up to 70 per cent at www.laterooms.com.

And, if you follow all the advice in this step and think of your own ways to live within your budget, you'll find that you have spare cash to treat yourself to a well-earned break (provided of course that you've worked your fingers to the bone). Once you have got on top of your financial situation you will never look back.

Predicting future costs in all areas of your life is one of the keys to being financially switched on. Planning for future expenses will allow you to avoid credit/loans/overdrafts and therefore save all your hard-earned income going straight to your creditors. If you find you have more going out than is coming in, the situation needs to be corrected BEFORE any further steps can be taken.

If you make sure that you always keep a tight grip on your finances, they will never drift out of control ever again. If you know you're in control, you won't ever be fearful of your financial situation again.

Remember to:

- Keep a record of future expenses, particularly big ones, and plan for them in advance

- If you must keep a credit card, use it to YOUR advantage following my advice; never abuse yourself by abusing the credit card!

- Check each expense on credit card and bank statements – banks and financial organizations do make mistakes and there is always a risk that someone has managed to get hold of your private details. Even the Government plays fast and loose with our financial data, as demonstrated by the bank details of 25 million people being lost in the post by a careless civil servant (just one example!)

- Keep an eye on loan and interest payments (if you still have them); switch when better rates are available

What we aim to have achieved by the end of this step is some breathing space in financial terms – some room to manoeuvre so that we are able to create some spare cash on a regular basis. This can then be filtered into savings. It may be a case of spotting opportunities once economies have been made, where cash-draining activities can be cut down or curtailed altogether. It really comes down to a question of priorities. Your first target could be to put aside 10 per cent of your income for savings. Once you're in a position to 'put aside', prepare to climb the next rung of the ladder that leads to riches.

STEP 12

DON'T LET YOUR MONEY JUST SIT THERE: DO SOMETHING!

Put not your trust in money, but put your money in trust.
Oliver Wendell Holmes

It may be unjust and unfair but the fact is that money goes to money. The rich get richer and the poor get poorer. Yes, it's unfortunate for those who have very little but once we accept it we are more likely to do something about it. Moaning about the injustices in life won't change them. To win we have to join in the game and follow the rules. The choice is ours.

So your first goal here is to set aside a small sum of money from which you can start making more money. With just £100 I will show you how to make a simple rock-solid investment with no risk attached. Setting money aside for investment is vital. Spending all the money you earn is never going to get you anywhere. Money breeds but only if it's cultivated correctly. It's a simple enough principle but it's astonishing how many people don't consider it essential.

I have come across thousands of people over the years who drift from month to month, year to year with no plan for their money and no definitive goals. They work like hamsters in a wheel, round and round, hoping for an improvement in their circumstances and before they know it they're at retirement age with very little to show for it.

Money left sitting in a current account earns nothing or next to nothing in interest and gets frittered away over time. It's a trap many people fall into. They get a little spare money together and they're not sure what to do with it so they do nothing. They waste time procrastinating as to whether they should invest in stocks and shares or whether to go for an ISA or high interest savings account and they end up leaving the money to stagnate, maybe in their current account, instead of taking action to make it work for them.

Most people feel that if their money is in a bank or building society, then it's safe but that isn't always the case. Any amount invested over £50,000 in the UK is currently not covered under the investors' compensation scheme so if you placed £1 million in a bank in this country and they happened to go out of business you would only get back a measly £50K and if you held any loans or mortgage debt with them they would reduce this instead of giving you back the cash!

With such a limited payout it's not surprising those unfortunate investors queued all day to retrieve their savings when news of the Northern Rock catastrophe hit the headlines. Worse anxiety followed for all those poor savers who chose a foreign-based bank like Icesave from Iceland, instead of a UK institution. Even our very own local authorities were victims, involving all of us! So, really, it's foolish for anyone to deposit a large amount of money with any one bank. That's why offshore bonds are very popular. They mostly offer enhanced protection against losses compared with onshore investments and have better protection than bank accounts.

There are a number of ways to help your money make money instead of relying on meagre handouts from high street banks. The trick is to be creative, then decide on a strategy and stick to it. It is a good idea to have some cash easily available, so think about how much you may need for emergency and keep it at home. I'm not talking about stashing hundreds of pounds under the mattress but maybe £100 in cash and then anything over and above this should be kept in a high interest instant access account at the very least. Short-term investments have their place, particularly as there is always a need to keep some money that you can access in the near future, should the need arise, but it wouldn't be sensible to leave it lying around in a low interest current account.

Even if you're unsure what to do with the money – make it work as hard for you as it can in its current location. Look at the highest rates with guarantees above the base rate, etc, or with introductory bonuses – review this and change when necessary. Your financial plans need to be razor sharp and you need to stick to them like glue. Don't be wishy-washy and indecisive, take action! Spend time researching the different options available to you or take independent financial advice. Visit www.unbiased.co.uk to find a local IFA. You can search by the postcode closest to work or home and even by the gender of the adviser you would like to see!

There are in fact a vast array of instant access accounts. If you don't bother to shop around for the best rates, effectively you lose money. The banks make enough from us already – why let them make any more? Get the best rate you can from them.

If you save in an account with a low rate of interest your cash will undoubtedly erode over time due to that old stumbling block: inflation. It's easy to forget the effect of inflation on savings. Try to bear in mind that it really means that money sitting in a savings account with an interest rate below that of inflation actually loses money over time, in real terms. Think of how much a balance of £10,000, for example, would have meant to your parents when they were young. In today's climate with the cost of living, etc, it's not even a decent deposit on a small flat. What we need to do is keep it working for us. Over the last ten years £10,000 placed in a poor paying account would be worth £11,605 when interest has been added. This sounds good initially as it's increased in value by £1,605 but the true value or buying power of this would be £9,068 in today's terms because of inflation. So whilst it's been sitting there, in real terms it's lost almost 10 per cent; 1 per cent per year.

One of the cornerstones of wealth building that the rich cultivate early on is an understanding of the need to rise above inflation. They understand the need to stay ahead of the game. They also appreciate the principle of compound interest. As we climb the steps you will be amazed at how quickly money can grow when using this principle. According to Albert Einstein, compound interest is the eighth wonder of the world and, 'the greatest mathematical discovery of all time'. Compound interest is the effect of adding the accumulated interest to the initial investment so that interest is earned, not just on the initial investment but the interest on it too. This results in a far higher interest amount being paid.

Let's say, for example, you invest a one-off sum of £1,000 in a high interest savings account for 20 years. For ease of calculation we'll assume you secure a return of 10 per cent. A simple interest calculation would lead you to believe that you would end up with £3,000 after 20 years (£1,000 @ 10 per cent x 20 years plus your £1,000 capital). But as Table 6 shows, with the snowball effect of compound interest factored in, you would do rather better than that.

Table 6: The real value of compound interest

Year	Investment	Interest	Year end value
1	£1,000	£100	£1,100
2	£1,100	£110	£1,210
3	£1,210	£121	£1,331
4	£1,331	£133	£1,464
5	£1,464	£146	£1,611
6	£1,611	£161	£1,772
7	£1,772	£177	£1,949
8	£1,949	£194	£2,144
9	£2,144	£214	£2,358
10	£2,358	£236	£2,594
11	£2,594	£259	£2,853
12	£2,853	£285	£3,138
13	£3,138	£314	£3,452
14	£3,452	£345	£3,797
15	£3,797	£380	£4,177
16	£4,177	£418	£4,595
17	£4,595	£459	£5,054
18	£5,054	£505	£5,560
19	£5,560	£556	£6,116
20	£6,116	£612	£6,727

In order to benefit from the effects of compound interest demonstrated above you need to:

* Save as much as you can for as long as you are able
* Don't withdraw early (compare the level of interest earned in the last 5 years compared to the first)
* Don't pull the interest out, keep it working for you

I hope you can also see how important it is to shop around

to get the best deal. A difference of 1 per cent in the interest rate paid may not seem all that significant but over periods of time the difference can prove to be substantial. For example, if you save £100 per month for just 10 years at an interest rate of 4 per cent and your savings compounded you would receive £14,717.62 and yet if you managed to secure a rate of 5 per cent your money pot would reach £15,499.21, a difference of £781.59 and over longer time frames the difference would be even more shocking!

So now I have you all fired up I want you to visit www.nsandi.com. Let's set the first stone in your wealth-building venture and you can have some fun as well.

As I mentioned at the beginning of this step, all you need to set off on your wealth-building venture is £100; premium bonds offer a unique way of saving and the minimum investment is only £100. You don't get paid interest but you have a chance of receiving a small prize regularly and an outside chance of a large sum of money from the monthly draws. They are a National Savings and Investments (NS&I) product and so offer a non risky form of saving; they are fully backed by HM Treasury which is worth its weight in gold these days.

Two £1 million tax-free prizes are 'won' in the monthly draw and a further one million in varying amounts, anything from £50 to £100,000.

The maximum investment is £30,000 and you must be a UK resident to invest. Premium bonds are an ideal investment; you can cash them in and access your money any time you wish as well.

Although monthly prizes are in no way guaranteed and can vary enormously, on average you should do no worse than 3 per cent per year. According to NS&I an investment of £30,000 could win 15 prizes a year. Bear in mind that inflation can erode your savings if 'luck' is not on your side but I think premium bonds are a worthwhile investment, particularly in the early days of wealth building since:

- Savings, backed by the UK Government!
- Your stake is safe, unlike when you buy a lottery ticket
- You have the heart-racing excitement of being in a draw with the possibility of big prizes but your stake is safe

So check out www.nsandi.com. With all National Savings and Investments, you can be safe in the knowledge that you're guaranteed 100 per cent of your money back plus any interest (other than equity bonds) because they are backed by the Government; see below for my top tips on the current best of the range.

Cash ISA – Save from £10 to £3,600 per year (over 16s only) in a tax-free account

Fixed Interest Savings Certificates – Invest £100 to £15,000 in each issue, tax-free with guaranteed interest rates

Index-Linked Savings Certificates – Again, from £100 to £15,000 in each issue, with returns guaranteed to beat inflation

Guaranteed Growth/Income Bonds – Invest £500 to £1 million. Interest is paid net. They offer a choice of fixed rate terms. You can choose which suits you best.

Guaranteed Equity Bonds – Investments from £100 to £30,000. This type of bond is linked to the FTSE100 and is a 5 year investment offering potential of impressive growth with no risk to capital

Remember with economic conditions as they are, finding a secure home for your money must come first. Then bring into play other factors such as interest rates.

Once you have made an initial investment you can enjoy the satisfaction of knowing that it is beginning to grow for you. When you have enough money in instant access accounts earning the best return you possibly can, then you can move up the ladder with the rest of your money. Start filtering some of your interest each month into regular savings accounts with better returns or even regular savings equity ISAs, etc. (You can currently save up to £7,200 each year in a stocks and shares ISA and not pay tax on the income. But if you also have a cash ISA for that year, the total amount invested in both ISAs must not exceed £7,200, and only £3,600 of the £7,200 can be invested in a cash ISA.)

Start saving regularly now and take advantage of the 10 per cent regular saver rates that are available as most banks look for new regular savers. (They see this as a good way of attracting new long-term clients.)

Points to remember:

- Open a number of different savings accounts and move savings around to follow the best rate. Banks and building societies continually change their savers' rates; you simply follow the highest. (Electronic banking means this isn't as painful as it used to be.)

- Shop around, do comparisons for all savings accounts, use a website to help you and/or speak to an independent financial adviser (IFA)

- Make a point of checking weekly. It soon becomes second nature and there's rarely a time when you won't come across a better deal elsewhere

STEP 13

MAKE MONEY AT HOME

*The gent who wakes up and finds himself a success
hasn't been asleep.*
Wilson Mizner

There can be lots of reasons why going out to work in a full-time job or setting up a business seems like an impossible task. Perhaps you are the parent of young children or are tied to the home for other reasons. These circumstances don't need to dictate the level of your income. There are many businesses that can be operated from home, fit around family commitments *and* provide great earning potential. The great thing about living in the twenty-first century is the variety of different options open to everyone; there are no limits, or far fewer than ever before.

Working from home is a perfect way for women (or men in the role of house-husband) to enjoy a career and still get to be there when the kids get home from school. It wasn't so long ago that a woman with ambition was shunned. Unfortunately, it may still be the case that successful women are sneered at by those who find it hard to accept their achievements, but despite them, the door is most firmly open for women to become wealthy. Back in the 1950s anything more than a little light typing outside of household chores would have been frowned upon.

A few years ago I was introduced by my sister Trina to her friend Doreen, who is now 75. She is a very talented artist; not just mediocre, she has a gift. As a child she loved to paint and dreamed of becoming an artist when she left school but her father was mortified at the very thought of his daughter earning money in this way and so he refused to allow her to follow her dreams. She went to secretarial school instead and obediently agreed to marriage as soon as a young man proposed, giving up all hope of ever using her talent and then spent forty years regretting her enforced decision. It's only when her father died that she felt free enough to get the brushes out once more and now she spends her days of retirement, painting to her heart's content. I think it's very sad that she wasn't able to do what she wanted; sad that her father cared more about what the neighbours thought than the fulfilment of his daughter's wishes. The good news is that you and I are able to follow our dreams and we will shrug off any sniggering at our attempts to fulfil our heart's desire. We won't give a thought to what the neighbours think.

Ironically, despite being held back by her desperation to please her parents, Doreen was very lucky in many ways. She had a gift which directed her towards her dream. There was no doubt in her mind what she wanted to do. So many people lack such a clear vision. There are so many choices available in our society and choice is confusing. Choice breeds inactivity. That's why so many people don't enjoy what they do for a living. Most end up blindly stumbling into a career not really knowing what they would love to do. Where for example are today's geniuses?

So what exactly can you do from home? If you feel

absolutely moved in a certain direction from the head and heart then, without a doubt, that is the route to follow. Forget everyone else's image of you. Forget your parents' wishes or urges towards a particular field. They're probably making attempts to graft their own unfulfilled ambitions onto you. Don't let them do it; they've had their chances. Carve your own niche. Don't live their idea of life instead of your own. You don't want to wake up one day at the end of someone else's life. Make your own choices. Don't live to please others.

If you have no direction that leaps to mind, don't despair; the list is endless. I will show you the most likely ways to achieve wealth and you can discover the most appealing option for yourself and your own circumstances.

It's a good idea to spend some time considering your choices. You may not be drawn seductively towards a particular path but most people find they have an inclination of one sort or another. Perhaps you have an affinity in a certain area.

So what exactly can you do from home? The list is endless but here are just a few ideas:

- Accountant
- Active investor
- Advertising agency
- Antiques dealer
- Hairdresser
- Private investigator

You needn't stick to just one either; you can combine child-minding with a laundry and ironing service or house-sitting with typing or writing, for instance.

And you can 'fill in' when you have time with other money-spinning opportunities that provide 'easy' income, money for old rope:

- Online auction site trader – This is something you can pick up and put down any time, so can be ideal for mums to fit around busy family life. You can pick up bargains while out shopping and resell online (make sure you research first to make sure you'll be selling cheap and still making a profit) or buy lost luggage from airlines. Thousands of suitcases are lost every year by travellers, and unclaimed baggage is auctioned off every now and then. You can pick up fantastic bargains this way and make a tidy profit

- Become a virtual assistant – When small businesses start out they often can't afford a full-time salary for secretarial or administrative support or sometimes bigger businesses can be snowed under and need temporary extra assistance. This is where you come in. You can advertise yourself and work from your home computer as an office assistant to any number of different companies. By advertising yourself you'll receive a better daily rate but if you prefer going through an agency you can expect to receive from £15 to £25 per hour – check outwww.allianceofukvirtualassistants.org. uk or www.virtualassistantjobs.com

- Become a doula – This is another 'filla' that's perfect for mums; a doula assists women before, during and after the birth of their child by cleaning, shopping, cooking, caring for the other children in the family or simply supporting the new mum. When the baby is born, a doula can offer care for the baby and support the mother. Experience as a mum is invaluable to some women who perhaps don't have close family members around and you can expect to make at least £5,000 per annum this way. Check out www.nurturing birth.co.uk or www.britishdoulas.co.uk

- Advertisements – Some companies will pay you between

£70 to £200 a month to advertise their business on the side of your car, depending on the size of the advert. This really is money for old rope since you do no more than tolerate it being there. It doesn't damage the bodywork and is easily removed – see www.adsoncars.com

- Questions for cash – There are companies that answer questions for cash. These companies offer a service where you text any question you need a quick answer to and they text back a comprehensive answer/solution. You might be stuck out somewhere, for example, and need the number of a travelling mechanic. The text answering services will text you whatever you need and they are always looking for researchers to help them answer the thousands of daily texts they receive. Become a researcher and answer questions for UK text answering services. You can make a fair amount of money this way and it's a flexible way to bring in extra income. Earnings are around £10 per hour and on a full-time basis you can earn around £20,000 to £25,000 yearly. If you want to test the system text a question to Texperts 66000, or ANSA 87199 – check www.texperts.com

Working from home offers great tax benefits and saves a great deal of money on premises, business rates, etc. It also means you'll be saving on commuting/motoring expenses too. Limitations are endless and that can be very liberating!

But staying at home doesn't mean you can have an extra hour in bed in the morning; it means you can start work an hour earlier. If you feel intimidated by the thought of going the whole hog, leaving your current job and diving into a home-based business, it is possible to dip your toe in the water first. Move on to the next step and I will show you how.

STEP 14

DON'T GIVE UP YOUR DAY JOB

Every exit is an entry somewhere.
Tom Stoppard

If what you want – and by now we have established that you do – is to make serious money, then relying on your day job to provide it is not always going to work, particularly if you are employed on basic salary and do not have any potential to earn promotion, bonus or commission. It's easy to slip into the habit of coming home from work and flopping, because at the end of the day it takes motivation to do anything else.

But if we want to get to grips with our finances and propel ourselves from being moderately comfortable to being wealthy, then we have to start doing things differently. We need to box clever. We need to relish the thought of a sideline business and look forward to getting home to work on it. And once the profits start to flow, it can be incredibly satisfying and rewarding to see the fruits of your labour begin to grow.

While many people turn up for their eight-hour shift, then forget all about work until just before their next shift, we are going to remain alert and focused. Their inactivity provides even greater opportunity for people like you and me. So heads up, we'll look past the salary waiting at the end of every month; our time and energy can be invested in alternative money-making strategies.

So many money-making opportunities can pass over your head if it's down, too busy concentrating on fulfilling the needs of your day job. Learning to remain alert and recognize the opportunities is one of the skills you need to learn in this step. Once you're in the habit of noticing opportunities you'll see them pop up all around you.

And even though we will be working on wealth creation strategies in this book, one of the best methods of wealth creation is to increase your income. Creating another source of revenue can double your household income within a year, provided it's a well thought-out strategy.

What I'm saying is that; say, for example, you were the owner of a burger bar, you might make a reasonable income from working and serving all day on your little patch. But how many owners would consider opening another burger bar in a lay-by a mile away? Better still how about having burger bars open all over town? If you were doing well with one outlet would that be your goal achieved?

I know it's a simple example but it makes perfect sense. It always pays to think big. Of course you can't serve in two burger bars in different locations and this brings difficult business decisions (but no one said it would be easy). You will need to find staff you can trust and that's not a breeze either. However, there are lots of good people out there. That's where your judgement comes in when you decide at the interview if they are right for you and you for them; it's a two-way street for sure.

Know where your talents lie. This applies to any business you're in – whether it's running a café or a financial institution. If you want the business to grow, you need the right staff.

It's so important to get the right people on your bus.

Ownership is important. It's where real money can be made (or lost!). There's nothing to stop you gunning for ownership of something while doing your regular 9 to 5 whether it's a burger bar or a website selling knitting patterns to the housebound and elderly. (Hey, that's a great idea, has anyone come up with that before? Zoe (my PA), make a note of that!) A good salary and company car are nice, a subsidized pension and private health insurance something else, but for some people it's just not enough. If you feel this way make sure you look at all of the options first. It's a tough world out there and timing of any new venture is so important.

Remember once you have set up your own business to expand into different areas that are not associated to each other in order to spread the risk. If you study the rise of any successful person you will see that a diverse business approach is one of the keys to his or her success. Most wealthbuilders haven't relied on one income stream to achieve their goals. Diversity is the key to unlock success. Do not put all your eggs in one basket.

STEP 15

FIND THE GOLDEN NUGGET

Between the idea/And the reality
Between the motion/And the act/Falls the Shadow
T S Eliot

Getting rich by accident, now there's a thing. The Golden Nugget is what I call that one genius idea or occurrence that changes everything. It's the switching on of the light bulb in your mind; that 'eureka' moment most of us experience at some time or another and do nothing about. We mull it over, think how marvellous it would be and then promptly forget all about it. Entrepreneurs seize that one moment and exploit it, turning it into something real.

Many of us have them; fabulous ideas that excite us. Most of us will do nothing about them. What you need to do now you're almost a third of the way through your climb is to think laterally and consider all possibilities available to you. The biggest rewards always go to those who choose to capitalize on a great idea. It doesn't even have to be your own idea. Having ideas doesn't pay the bills, executing them does. If you make moves to build an empire from one small nugget, you'll be the one whose pockets will be lined, not the person who thought up the idea in the first instance. No one makes money from an idea unless they capitalize on it. One of the first rules before going into business on the back of a good idea is to make sure you protect the execution of it and obtain a trademark for the production of it, or someone will steal it from you. Of course, you'll always have competition but that's just a case of staying ahead of the game.

The unusual is often where fortunes are made, be it an unusual idea or product or line of work you are offering; one of the wealthiest men I know made his fortune by clearing up after the dead. If someone dies and is not found for a while or if someone is murdered, it gets messy. It's ugly and upsetting and, I'm told, the stench is almost unbearable. This chap arrives once the police have done their job and blitzes the place, 'cleaning up' afterwards and I mean this in both senses. He gets paid big money because what he does is unpleasant.

He started off as a one-man band and now has a team of dedicated professionals with strong stomachs. He saw the value in choosing an unpopular business; one that hoards of people would not be drawn to and almost guaranteed success for himself. He started out with very little competition. It was a niche market, and consequently he was able to name his price. He appeared at the door of local council offices, like the pied piper, offering his much needed services and, naturally, he was able to call the tune. Not very glamorous I'll admit but that's precisely why it's so lucrative.

He is now considering selling his business and will make enough capital to retire at the ripe old age of 35 and is already asking for my help and advice to investigate a new avenue he can build an enterprise around. That is how many millionaires have made their fortunes. Not by inheritance, stocks and shares or income, but by selling their companies once they have built them.

It may appear, from the array of magazines and newspapers on the shelves, that the way to make a million is to become a celebrity or sports star but it is most certainly not the case. I think it's such a pity that the young clamour for this kind of life in desperation of the glossy lifestyle it seems to bring with it. The fact is that celebrities and the like amount to less than three out of every 100 millionaires in America. The likelihood is that lusting after this kind of life will get you nowhere. It's far more likely that fortunes will be made in the business arena than on the stage. This is the reason I feel sorry for the young children who spend their day dreaming of being a celebrity because their real chance is in the world of business if only they knew it!

Your golden nugget could be just waiting around the corner for you: that idea, brainwave, or maybe it comes from something you haven't even considered as an asset before now – for example if you have a garage that is going to rack and ruin. Some people find they can earn a fair income each month by renting out small spaces that they never even considered of any value, except maybe as a place to store junk.

It is alleged that Charlie Thompson, a sales rep for a sweet company, in 1899 (so the story goes) dropped a tray of samples he was showing a prospective client. While he scrambled to rearrange them, the client apparently marvelled at the mixture and thus the Liquorice Allsort was born.

Some people have started out with ideas and have been surprised at the phenomenal success they've achieved, far exceeding their expectations. Take Alex Tew for example; he wanted to be a millionaire and decided that all he had to do to get a million dollars was sell a million items for just $1 each. He realized that a large webpage has one million pixels so he set out to sell each pixel in small blocks to advertisers for $1 per pixel. You can see the result of his efforts at www.million-dollarhomepage.com. His idea was startlingly simple but nevertheless it worked like a dream. He achieved his ambition of becoming a millionaire by following through on his idea – ingenious.

Mark Zuckerberg, the founder of Facebook, the online social network, is now a billionaire. He was just 23 years old when he came up with the idea. It is an entrepreneur's paradise with the right ideas!

If you're lacking ideas it is worth reading up on how the rich have made their money. You may find some inspiration from the ideas of others. If there is someone you admire who has achieved the sorts of things you dream of achieving, find out how they did it. Read about them to find out what motivated them and how they found the inner drive to reach their goals. It may help you to identify what motivates you as a person. What drives one person may not have any effect on another.

It's even better if you can enlist the help of people you know or perhaps have contact with who have achieved success in their chosen fields. If you approach them and tell them of your plans, they may be happy to give you some advice and encourage-ment; it's a big compliment you're giving them after all and often successful people admire the efforts of others. Mentoring has been used since ancient times, in China, Greece and other great civilizations, to develop leaders and assist young people on the right path. By recognizing the value that mentors have in developing new skills, you can harness what you learn and pass it on to your own employees if and when you have them. Many forward-thinking businesses are now recognizing the benefits of mentoring young employees and encouraging them to take the lead.

Discovering the many different ways people have found success can be inspirational and can help you to trust in your own ability to make dreams come true. If you learn to trust your instincts once proven, you will gain in confidence and develop plans around them and push your ideas into action. If you have a sudden flash of inspiration, then go with it. Put your idea down on paper and start to develop a plan around it. So many fantastic ideas fall by the wayside because people don't follow through and see them to fruition.

You'd be surprised how many people made themselves extremely wealthy simply by following through on one single moment of inspiration. I find mind mapping a useful tool in bringing shape to my ideas. Mind mapping is a powerful technique, especially useful if you're like me and prefer both to 'see' and read information. Seeing is believing and looking at your ideas on paper allows you to make the best use of your brain power.

You can form a logical pathway from your initial idea to execution by making use of mind mapping. A mind map is a brainstorming diagram based on an idea. It gives form to an idea, giving structure and allowing it to take shape in your mind. Putting ideas on paper in a structured format also aids problem solving.

I will show you an example of mind mapping and how useful it can be in giving shape to your ideas. Let's say, for instance, that you are lying in the bath one evening and at the sight of the bubbles an idea pops into your head to offer a car washing service at your local supermarket. You may not know the first thing about setting up a service like this and all your thoughts will be jumbled together. The complications of executing your idea may seem overwhelming and by the time the bathwater begins to cool you've shelved yet another possible golden nugget.

What you should do is jump out of the bath, run to grab a pen and paper and prepare a mind map. The central idea goes in the middle and then you use words and pictures to develop your idea. I like to use circles to ring-fence projects and develop further ideas within the project itself. Fig. 2 is just an example.

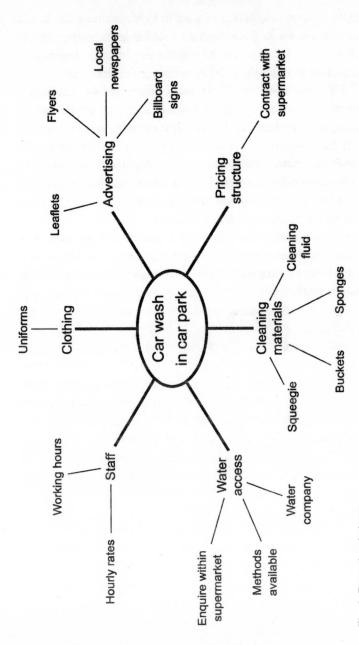

Fig. 2: Example mind map

Use different colours and texts to help stimulate the brain. The human mind finds reams of bland text boring; bright colours and shapes excite and energize the brain and encourage free thinking. When preparing a mind map, always work in landscape as this is more conducive to the brain's natural preferences; we are attuned to seeing in landscape.

Seeing your ideas taking shape on paper can provide you with the confidence you need to take it to the next level and implement them. You'll never regret the efforts you make to grasp at the golden nugget in your mind and make it real. By formulating your plans on paper you break each step of the process down into manageable circles. Little by little, step by step, you'll turn your idea into a plan and your plan will become a business and in five years' time you could be selling that business on for a tidy sum. That magic moment is waiting just for you!

STEP 16

MAKE THE RIGHT IMPRESSION

The most important single ingredient in the formula of success is knowing how to get along with people.
Theodore Roosevelt

Whatever the circumstances, however testing your client, customer, patient, partner, remain professional at all times. That is your personal mantra and it is one of the most important rules when it comes to being successful. When those around you lose their cool it is paramount that you remain the gentleman/woman at all times. Be determined, yes. Be ruthless in the business sense of the word if you have to, but always remain courteous, temperate and refined in all your dealings. Good manners cost nothing, a sentiment that sometimes appears to be long since dead. It's something my grandmother used to say but it's still every bit as true now as it was in a bygone era. Ignore it at your peril. Being rude may cost you dearly.

Deal with all people you come into contact with through your business with respect and they will always come back. I know from personal experience that this is so. Have honour in all your dealings and people will trust you. You may have to forgo a quick buck but it pays dividends in the long run; I can attest to that.

Customer service is everything, in my opinion. One of the main focuses in my company is making sure we give our clients what they need. I believe it is crucial to the success of any business, whether it be running a restaurant or a local corner shop.

In many sectors of business in this country I believe the standards of service are appalling. Providing a professional service is the key to customer satisfaction which in turn is paramount; it is fundamental to securing the future of any business.

Another golden rule and key to remaining professional is to have a professional appearance and ensure you never look poor; however poor you are, do your best not to look it. If you appear to be scruffy, then you won't be treated with respect. If you look like you haven't made an effort with your appearance, you may give the impression of laziness. If you want to be seen as powerful and in control, then stride along looking confident and self-assured, with what our ancestors called 'the look of the eagles'. Self-confidence is a priceless asset to take into a business meeting. Whatever business you go into and whoever you are dealing with, remaining professional is the key to success. Stride to give the appearance that you're someone who should be followed. If you appear to be weak, needy and desperate, you will be treated that way and will be easily dismissed.

And, however much we may dislike the fact, looks do matter. First impressions are often crucial in projecting an overall image of yourself. If the first thing clients notice about you is your grubby appearance, it will take an awful lot of smart talking to convince them otherwise. I'm not suggesting you blow all you've saved hard for to purchase an expensive suit; it's all about the overall image you project. Search the sales for a decent suit. (This advice applies to both men and women; nothing is more attractive or instils more confidence than a smart, well turned out man or woman.) Or even trawl some of your local charity shops; there are often suits available there and if they fit well they'll look smart enough, provided they're clean and pressed. Dress as if you're worth a million dollars and it's very likely people will treat you that way. It is essential that you remain well-groomed at all times. Stick to elegance and simple sophistication and you won't go wrong.

As soon as you begin to take on employees make sure they understand how much emphasis you place on personal standards. There are bosses who are perfectly happy for their staff to stroll around the office in 'scruffs' but I'll never be one of them. I'm sure it's all very relaxed when staff turn up in tracksuits and jeans but are they as productive, do they value the work place, do they feel as good about themselves? Does it inspire confidence in clients/investors to see your staff loafing around as if it's a day off? I don't believe it does.

I always send staff home if they are dressed inappropriately. Indeed I sent one member of staff home to change because she turned up at the office in flip-flops. She complained that it was too hot for shoes! I said, 'Flip-flops look great . . . on the beach!' Respect the work place and it will be a far better place. I always respect my staff and enjoy their company; I am certain they all know ultimately I'm there (as all directors should be) to make good decisions at the right time for the benefit of the whole company.

Part of looking good is dressing appropriately so that you fit in. Try to adapt to the situation you're going into. If you fit in with people it affirms their positive perception of you and sends a message that you are like them. You don't have to be a stunner to look great; it's all about confidence. Good looks appeal to everyone, it's simple human nature, but self-assurance tips the scales. Being confident and comfortable in your own skin overcomes most flaws.

If you feel good about yourself it is so much easier to project confidence and cultivate immediate trust in other people. In business it is so important to gain the trust of others and if you can manage to do this you will be in a position to manoeuvre almost any circumstances to suit you. When you meet people for the first time, be it your bank manager, client, business colleague, even a prospective lover, you have such a small window of opportunity to 'click' with them and although first impressions are formed in an instant the effects are far-reaching and often impact far more on the outcome of the deal than we appreciate.

Human beings sing off the same hymn sheet when it comes to initial encounters and most people base their decision on whether they like a person on the briefest of interactions. The key to making a positive impression is to set the mood on arrival. You have power from a distance; harness it. Aim to make anyone you meet feel comfortable but also impressed. Even before you open your mouth it is possible to give an impression of strength and capability.

The presence you emit influences the way others perceive you and I will tell you how to do it so that you instantly command respect and build rapport. It's something that should be taught in schools since it is a critical asset necessary to succeed in life, but sadly it is not part of the curriculum.

A first impression allows strangers the briefest insight into you and your life and because they have only limited information to base an assessment of you on they assume that the 'whole' you is condensed into that one short moment. If, when you first meet people you are jolly and happy, they will assume you are always like that. Initial information 'given off' in a first impression is weighted far more heavily than anything that comes later. If you engage in the first few minutes as a warm, honest, positive person that is the lasting impression you will leave your 'audience' with.

Everyone, almost without exception, believes they are a good judge of character and therefore, however badly you behave subsequently, people who have a positive first impression of you will search for traits in you that confirm their initial assessment was correct, even to the point of ignoring behaviour that doesn't 'fit' their impression of you. No one likes to admit they're wrong. It's an unconscious phenomenon and one we can use to our advantage in the world of business.

You may not realize it but the effect you have on the way others feel can be very powerful. When you engage with people it is important that you leave them feeling good about themselves. Moods are infectious.

If you're feeling tense in a situation or first meeting it is easy to be distracted by your own feelings and forget to tap into the other person's needs. Tapping into and building an understanding of the way others feel when they talk to you is the secret to making a positive first impression. Put your own feelings to the back of your mind and be generous to others.

By doing this you automatically become 'desirable' and what you're offering becomes more appealing. Learning to work with the dynamics of human relationships and social exchange immediately puts you 'in the money'. It is a paradox but providing others with what they need is the shortest route to getting what you want. Think of it as laying the groundwork for reciprocation.

So, in summary, my seven golden rules to making a successful first impression are:

- Appreciate – aim to make people feel appreciated; everyone loves to feel accepted. Find a quality in someone you genuinely admire (don't be fake or they'll see through you) and compliment it

- Connect – find common ground to make others feel a connection with you. Say something like, 'Yes, I feel the same,' or 'I like that too,' or 'Oh yes, you're like me in that way'. It's not difficult to find small things to agree on and it generally sets people at ease

- Elevate – people like to feel happy and most people are drawn towards jolly characters. Be a bit playful and humorous (when and if appropriate); it can work wonders

- Enlighten – everyone likes to learn new things. If you can be enthusiastic about your subject and demonstrate knowledge you will give the impression of being stimulating and appealing

- Show interest – be open and available. Acknowledge efforts to engage with you. Nod, smile and ask genuine questions. People are highly attuned to others if real interest is shown in them

- Make eye contact – this will give out positive vibes and show that you are approachable

- Always be honest and sincere – if you are false, it will be noticed

Stick to these guidelines and you won't go far wrong in setting an ideal scene for negotiation which I'll talk about in the next step. Of course, in business terms, the first and, probably only, physical contact you'll experience is the handshake. It's a common ritual but has a big impact and gives weight to a positive first impression, provided it's not weak and feeble. A firm handshake projects the impression of strength and vigour and the more complete the grip the more warmth and confidence exudes from you. 'Feminine' handshakes, even from a woman, are less favourable and give the impression of a weak character.

And, finally, in all your dealings, play your top trump card and be true and honest!

STEP 17

CULTIVATE THE ART OF SELLING

It is not that pearls fetch a high price because men have dived for them; but on the contrary men dive for them because they fetch a high price.
Richard Whateley, Introductory Lectures on Political Economy

Selling is an art, or a skill at the very least. Some people are born to sell. They take to it like a duck to water, it's in their blood. They enjoy it, delight in lining up their target then going in for the kill, savouring their victory and feasting on the, often ample, rewards that follow.

Others find it a little more difficult, it's not a skill that comes naturally to them. But all of us sell every day, often without even realizing it. Most of us have been in a situation where we need to sell something, however small. Maybe even a car or house. In the sports arena the ability to sell, both on and off the field, is an important part of the strategies used; the captain of a team sells himself to his team mates to motivate them and engender team spirit.

Political parties sell to the voters, they sell their manifesto. The prime minister puts himself on the market for election by the party. Even countries sell themselves to foreign visitors via tourist information, etc. Life is one big circle of selling. Once we become comfortable with this fact we can join the game, form a strategy and put ourselves in the position of winners.

Without the ability to sell we have little chance of succeeding, no matter what we choose to do. We all come across many situations when the need for selling ourselves arises, often without even being aware. On a daily basis at work, for example, we may have interviews with colleagues and managers. We are far more likely to receive a promotion if we sell ourselves well. Sales techniques are of benefit to managers in the work place; successful managers motivate their team by providing reassurance and selling the benefits of supporting the structure.

The good news is that sales technique can be learnt. If you're not a natural there are many 'tricks' to be learnt that can help you to become competent and ultimately successful. Selling is the bedrock of success. To make money you have to do one of three things:

- Sell yourself
- Sell your skills/knowledge/ideas/time
- Sell a commodity of some sort

Learn to sell well and the sky's the limit.

So let's turn to the first: the art of selling yourself. Learning to sell yourself can transform the circumstances you find yourself in, both in your private and professional life. A confident, positive approach has a ripple effect throughout many if not all aspects of life and can often see people through the most challenging of times.

You will then find that you're on top of your game by marketing yourself to your full potential when an exciting new relationship appeals to you. Relationships involve selling, even if only at first to a prospective partner. If you're selling yourself it may be that you need to work on building your confidence first.

An important factor when aiming to conquer this step is to master the psychology of selling yourself. If you are able to like yourself as a person and reinforce self-belief, then you can reach the stage where you think that you are selling the best thing since sliced bread. You need to start believing that what you have to offer is of value. But don't worry if you are not there yet – we can start the ball rolling with a few practical examples. The next time you go to say, 'I can't', stop yourself and say, 'I shall give it my very best' and set your mind to focus on the best outcome for the given situation. This will have the positive ripple effect, not only personally but for the people around you.

Never let failure get you down. If you feel you haven't achieved what you set out to immediately, just move the goalposts a little so that you can see your efforts as a movement towards success. You may be lacking some skills but they will develop with practise. To be successful in sales you need to be:

- A good listener
- Optimistic
- Solution focused
- Goal orientated
- Persuasive
- Flexible
- Sociable
- Confident
- Persistent

The most important quality from the list above is, I believe, optimism. The optimist believes that things will turn out well. They bring a positive outlook to all situations and this has a positive effect which increases the chances of a positive outcome. Consequently they become yet more optimistic! They get stuck in a spinning wheel of good fortune. Surround yourself with optimistic people; optimism is both therapeutic and infectious.

You may find that, when working on this step, aspects of your character you haven't always been happy with may improve. If it's your skills/knowledge, ideas or time that you're selling, you'll need to brush up on your negotiation techniques to ensure that you don't undersell yourself. Once you learn the skill of effective negotiation, you will benefit, not only financially, but by overspill into other areas of your life, perhaps with family or friends or your partner.

Each time you manage to close a deal, you will feel more confident and capable, and the power will help you to lose self-conscious doubts. The key to gaining confidence is practice, practice, practice. It's just like learning something off by heart; it seems impossible at first but with practice it becomes second nature.

Before you negotiate a deal it's a good idea to draw on the lessons you learnt from Step 7, visualizing the people involved, their voices, their responses to you; every detail of the meeting. Imagine stepping into the shoes of a trained negotiator, an accomplished salesperson. 'See' the events going your way, everything slipping into place. Feel yourself in a strong position, gaining ground. View each negotiation not as a battle but more a game, one that you intend to win. You'll find it can be a profound learning experience. In effect what you're doing is teaching your unconscious mind to emulate the responses of a first-class negotiator.

Negotiation is, in effect, a conversation that leads to an

agreement. Keep it low-key, remain cool, don't appear overly-excited. Sell like you don't need the money. Just focus on the outcome you hope to achieve. It's all about getting the other person to see that agreeing with you is ultimately going to be better for everyone. All the best business deals are a 'Win Win' situation all round!

When it comes to selling a product or commodity of some sort, it's a good idea to believe in what you're selling. Genuine enthusiasm is infectious so the best tactic is to sell something you really feel passionate about. It's not always necessary as there are some who can sell 'snow to Eskimos' and if you're one of those people you can skip my words of advice and propel yourself forwards onto the next step.

One absolute must when buying to sell is to research your market. Make sure someone will want to buy before you lay out any capital. I recently watched the film *In Pursuit of Happiness*, a story based on true-life events in which Chris Gardner, a struggling salesman from San Francisco, played by Will Smith, breaks one of the most important rules in business: he buys a stack load of x-ray scanners in the belief that they will sell like hot cakes. Before testing the market, he spends the only capital he has. He fills his flat with the useless stock and then realizes no one is interested in buying them. As a result he becomes bankrupt and loses his girlfriend into the bargain. With no job, no home and no woman he has to try and build a future for himself and his five-year-old son. He decides that stockbroking is a way of making it big and in an effort to break into that world he joins an unpaid but brutally competitive stockbroker training programme. He has not a dollar to his name and resorts to sleeping on the streets and even in the toilet of a railway station. After a long struggle he eventually rises above all the obstacles becoming a huge success. He made millions as a result of his true grit and sheer determination. Three morals to this story:

- Never buy to sell without analysing the market thoroughly first
- Timing in any business transaction is crucial; what sells like hot cakes one year may dive the year after, then make a miraculous come-back five years later
- If you enter a bad patch keep focused and take a fresh look at where you are; stay positive and never sell your integrity

Whichever path you choose to take, whatever you choose to sell, using the technique of focus will give you the best opportunity to achieve your goals. People have often said to me that I am single-minded, positive and focused. They ask me if this helped me in achieving my goals. I strongly believe it does help in addition to visualize how you'll feel when you attain what you set out to. It also helps to feel how it would be if you did not reach your goal. Feeling the end result in our grasp is a very powerful factor. This can be applied to everything one wants in life. Much has been made recently of football managers who call in psychologists to help teams improve their performance (results) by positive thinking. I very much believe in positive thinking but it's wise to be mindful of the fact that eleven players from the local pub will not beat the might of Arsenal (yes, my team). Being realistic in your aspirations is important to help you on the road to success. I'm not suggesting that one aims too low. In fact, aiming high is much more exciting and brings bigger rewards.

Always be mindful that negativity is extremely unproductive and draws in a negative aura. Positive is just as it sounds: it's forward, ambitious and exciting and sends pulses of magnetic fever everywhere. In between these two is sitting on the fence which is wishy-washy, boring and insipid. Remember that people who are positive thinkers inspire not only themselves but others as well.

Whatever position you find yourself in as you read, you can

change your destiny if you become a confident salesperson and harness the power of positive thinking, I promise you. Doors will open that before seemed shut, opportunities will arise that before were not seen. As with all human beings there will be problems that need dealing with along your journey, but what a satisfying feeling to be admired rather than searching to admire. Once you have conquered the psychology of selling you will have mastered one of the most important arts needed to tread the road to riches.

STEP 18

RUN A TIGHT SHIP EVEN IN HARD TIMES

Keep your thoughts positive because your thoughts become your words. Keep your words positive because your words become your behaviours. Keep your behaviours positive because your behaviours become your habits. Keep your habits positive because your habits become your values. Keep your values positive because your values become your destiny.

Gandhi

I don't want to start this step on a downer but let's get the bad news out of the way early on; if you take a look at the figures for the number of new businesses that fail in their first year you'll feel a sliver of razor-sharp ice scrape down your spine. It's not encouraging reading. And no, I'm not going to quote the figures here because it will only serve to undermine all the good work you've done so far in building motivation and confidence. I mention it only to remind you that once you've created an income stream you need to pull out all the stops to keep it healthy and thriving.

The good news is that the present economic climate is not

hostile to new ventures as it was thirty years ago (even with the credit crunch). Until the late 1980s the word 'private' was a dirty word when it came to business. Before 'the iron lady' came to power Britain remained in the stranglehold of the unions and nationalized industries ruled the day. The UK became known as the 'Sick Man of Europe'.

Mrs Thatcher released the grip of the unions and began the process of denationalization of major industries. She brought competition back, encouraging free competition and private enterprise which from a financial point of view is spot on!

I just hope that 'competition' doesn't become a dirty word in business again as it has in schools. It seems that the powers that be are intent on eliminating competitive attitudes in the young. Why? Life is a competition, and business certainly is; without it we may as well be living in a dictatorship.

So how can we make sure that new ventures compete with the best? The answer is to take positive action. To make sure your enterprise, whatever it may be, stays open for business, and to gain every chance to succeed, it is important to trim costs, keeping them as low as possible without risking a collapse of quality. It's important not to just cut costs willy-nilly though, anyone can do that. It involves careful analysis to identify weak spots and leaks. Find the right balance between profit and costs and remember to keep enough profit back for the future.

Points to remember when your business is in its infancy:

- Keep overheads to an absolute minimum
- Don't pay yourself if you can possibly get away with it. If you must take a salary, then only draw enough to feed and clothe yourself (and any dependants!)
- Make sure your debtors pay you in a timely manner
- Always pay your staff on time
- Turn lights and computers off at the end of the day

And once you've been going a while:

- *Still* keep overheads to a minimum
- Reinvest some of your profits
- Never compromise on quality or customer service
- Keep a close eye on your accounts; things can change quickly
- Be open and honest in your dealings with others including staff
- Don't rest on your laurels, keep focused at all times
- Love the business you're in – if you lose your passion for it, sell and do something you'll enjoy

One of the most recent valuable tools to get a fledgling business off to a flying start are the new wave of business networking websites. Previously only popular within the confines of the school playground, social networking is now commonplace in the office and professional practices.

Its infiltration has little to do with the loneliness of boardroom members; it's all about benefiting from the wealth of contacts and business opportunities rife among business online networks. Make use of www.ecademy.com or www.bttrade space.com. You can build your business profile online and exchange messages with other users. For more information or business support try www.webwednesdays.com or www.word ofmousenetwork.com. You'll be able to make contact with other professionals, who perhaps share the same problems (and hence solutions) as you. Exchanging ideas, making recommendations and referring clients between each other is a brilliant way of keeping afloat, especially when times are hard and in any event in the period when trying to build a business.

You can bounce ideas off like-minded people and benefit from mentors who may, perhaps, be further along the line than you, in terms of experience. You can find endless business opportunities online and perhaps even link in with someone in the same field as yourself, combining talents, experience and possibly even businesses. It can often be the best way to find a business partner.

Remember: if you do need to find a partner or the need to bring others into the business in order to obtain capital that you can't get any other way, make sure you keep hold of the majority share. Don't part with a major part of the equity; running a business is all about keeping control. If you lose the majority voting shares, even if it's only 1 per cent anything can happen to the dream you've worked so hard to make reality:

• The business can be sold from under your feet
• Merger with another company
• You could be ousted before you get a chance to empty your desk

At some point in running your business, if you are to become really successful, you are going to need to employ staff. It's not always easy to go from a one-man band to an employer and for some the transition can be a bit rocky.

See my tips below:

• Pick the best people; it's worth it for sure!

• Be clear about what you want them to do and how much they will get paid for doing it

• Try to inspire loyalty in your staff by being loyal to them – talk openly with them

• Be fair in your dealings with staff

- Set a good example

- Praise their good work and be honest with the things they need to improve; they will respect you for it and you will help to develop their careers (hopefully with you)

- Pay them a fair wage for the work they do and build in a bonus system. As soon as you can afford, start a company pension scheme; it's proven that staff feel appreciated and stay longer when they are members of a scheme, particularly if the employer pays the contributions

- Learn to trust them

- Recognition is always received well. If they've gone that extra mile for you, the least you can do is show your appreciation. People are always motivated to perform at their best if they feel appreciated and involved

- Fire non-achievers, lazy employees, anyone with a bad attitude. They're not good for the team morale and will hold you back

- Training and the prospect of progression are good for everyone. They bring the feel-good factor and will also benefit your company by increased sales and or higher professional standards

- Set an example – if your staff see you turning up late or ordering a pizza and lounging with your feet up on the desk don't be surprised if they do the same tomorrow

- Always support your managers in front of the rest of your staff. They work hard for you; show them respect!

- Fast-track talent

Finally, one of the biggest nails in the coffin of the vast majority of fledgling businesses is ignorance of the importance of cash flow. Lack of cash flow spells doom to any enterprise, no matter what the business entails. Running out of cash means that the business races along out of control like a runaway train. No matter how hard you run, you'll never catch up if you ignore the management of cash.

If you don't know the first thing about management accounting, you should find a good accountant. It will pay dividends in the long run. Sometimes, as the owner of a new enterprise, you can become so caught up with bringing new business in the door that the mundane (but critical) elements of running a business fly out of the window. If you constantly put financial issues on the back-burner, it will come back to bite you sooner or later, probably sooner. You'll find the taxman, landlord or disgruntled employees knocking on your door rather than new clients or, worse still, a bailiff with a court order.

Ignore cash flow at your peril. Stick to the basic rules of running a tight ship and the business you've created will prosper.

Now let's move onto the next step and find out how to protect what we've built.

STEP 19

PROTECT YOURSELF

He is rich or poor according to what he is,
not according to what he has.
Henry Ward Beecher

If you've built an income of say 30k and your income remains steady or increases, then a third of a million and possibly more will pass through your hands over the next ten years. It would be folly to use all of the steps in this book to promote and increase your financial health without ensuring that you would still be able to keep at least the same financial position if you were unfortunate enough to suffer an uncontrollable event. In this step we will look at common sense ways to protect you and your family, so that you can rest assured that all of your hard work and spoils will not be lost.

I will show you the safety nets you need to set up to protect yourself and your family. We are building on substance, not living by a hope, a wing and a prayer. Losing everything you've worked so hard to achieve would be disastrous but it can and does happen. It's so easy to be carried away with the pressures of a busy life and time can slip by without paying any attention to protecting what you've got. Building on wealth is great but it's so important to take good care of what you've already created.

Protection comes in many forms. You can insure your life so your family or business partner will be provided for in the worst case scenario, receive a large payment if diagnosed with a critical illness, cover your regular income should you fall ill and not be able to work or if you are made redundant. We have no control over certain events befalling us but we can affect the outcome by protecting ourselves financially. Make sure you prepare a shelter for any potential storm.

Life assurance

Life assurance is all too often put to the back-burner, despite compelling reasons to make it a priority; it is estimated that one in three adults don't have any life assurance. If tragedy strikes where is the fall-back position for the struggling family left behind? Again, it's something most people shelve for another day, but sometimes that day never comes, at least not until it's too late.

Do something about it now. Don't make your enduring legacy leaving a poverty-stricken family behind. And make sure what you do leave behind is adequate. It should be enough to pay off your mortgage completely and leave a lump sum so that the remaining family doesn't have to sell the home just to make ends meet. If the surviving partner has to care for young children he or she may not be able to work as well – where is money for food, clothes, heating and the occasional trip to the seaside going to come from?

Life cover doesn't cost the earth, but it's worth shopping around. Seek advice from an Independent Financial Adviser who will do all this work for you. There are various types of life cover. We shall look at the most popular of the main covers available:

- Term assurance – This is a fixed sum which is only paid out if the insured person dies within the term chosen. You can ask for the cover to increase with inflation, however your premiums will also rise. It's important to remember that when the term of the policy ends, the policy becomes worthless

- Decreasing term assurance is the same as above but reduces over the term – This is often used therefore to cover the outstanding balance on a mortgage; usually if interest rates stay below 10 per cent, the life cover is adequate to clear the outstanding balance on death

- Family income benefit – Another term assurance that pays out a fixed agreed amount on the death of the insured person every month or year until the end of the term. This is an ideal solution for anyone with young children as the surviving partner can use this to pay the bills or even school fees

- Whole of life – This policy covers you for the whole of your life (just like it says on the tin . . .), even if you live to see 120 years. Part of the policy includes an investment and so there will be a surrender value should you decide to pull the plug. This cover is often used for Inheritance Tax Planning (IHT)

Critical illness insurance
This provides a lump-sum payout if you are unlucky enough to suffer from any of the illnesses the policy specifies. The benefit of this cover is that you decide how the payout is used; for example, you may pay off your mortgage or invest the money to provide an income or even use the money to provide the very best in health care.

Fact: 1 in 3 people develop cancer some time in life (source: Cancer Research). Also before you finish the next chapter of this book 49 people will die but 139 will be diagnosed with a critical illness.

So now we are armed with the facts and figures let's look at what is covered by the typical policy.

- Alzheimer's disease – resulting in permanent symptoms
- Aorta graft surgery – for disease
- Aplastic anaemia – requiring regular blood transfusions
- Bacterial meningitis – resulting in permanent symptoms
- Benign brain tumour – resulting in permanent symptoms
- Blindness – permanent and irreversible
- Cancer – excluding less advanced cases
- Cardiomyopathy – of specified severity
- Coma – resulting in permanent symptoms
- Coronary artery bypass grafts – with surgery to divide the breastbone
- Creutzfeldt-Jakob disease (CJD) – resulting in permanent symptoms
- Deafness – permanent and irreversible
- Heart attack – of specified severity
- Heart valve replacement or repair – with surgery to divide the breastbone
- HIV infection – caught from a blood transfusion, a physical assault or at work
- Kidney failure – requiring dialysis
- Liver failure – end stage
- Loss of hands or feet – permanent physical severance
- Loss of independent existence – resulting in permanent symptoms
- Loss of speech – permanent and irreversible
- Major organ transplant
- Motor neurone disease – resulting in permanent symptoms

- Multiple sclerosis – with persisting symptoms
- Open heart surgery – with surgery to divide the breastbone
- Paralysis of limbs – total and irreversible
- Parkinson's disease – resulting in permanent symptoms
- Pre-senile dementia – resulting in permanent symptoms
- Progressive supranuclear palsy – resulting in permanent symptoms
- Stroke – resulting in permanent symptoms
- Third degree burns – covering 20 per cent of the body's surface area
- Traumatic head injury – resulting in permanent symptoms

As you can see, the list is very comprehensive. The key point is that if you are diagnosed with a covered condition and make a full recovery (however quick) the policy will still pay out and you can save or spend as you please.

Some critical illness policies even provide free cover for any children up to certain limits. However, remember that they all have different wording as to the exact nature of the illness and when the policy would in fact pay out. It is very important to take independent financial advice (from an IFA) when choosing the correct critical illness policy for you!

Income protection
Income protection policies are a wise choice. What would you rather do – forgo the odd glass of wine or two a week, or risk losing your home? The choice is easy when you look at it in those terms and yet so many people put the need to protect themselves low on their list of priorities. During the first half of 2007 the number of people losing their home as a result of an inability to keep up mortgage payments surged by almost a third. Protection can form a desperately needed

cushion against unplanned eventualities so putting money aside each month for income protection should be one of your top priorities. It's best to work on the principle that we all at some point may need to take three to six months off work and aim to provide adequate income saved in an emergency fund or have in place a protection policy that would cover this time period so that it is possible to survive without making too many sacrifices to your current lifestyle.

Imagine that you've worked so hard in your climb only to be knocked down a few steps or, worse still, knocked off altogether. To have to rely on state benefits is a come-down after you've had a taste of a better life. All it takes is a little effort and a small amount set aside each month and you can rest easy, leaving you free to concentrate on the business of wealth building.

- Income protection – A policy that provides an income (chosen at outset) over the selected term. You can choose a deferment period where the policy does not pay out, say, for the first month. This in turn will reduce the cost. The life office cannot cancel this cover if they get wind of the fact that you are in poor health; a different name for this, therefore, is permanent health insurance (PHI)

- Redundancy cover – This cover is for people who are employed. Should they be made redundant it pays a monthly income set at commencement of the plan. It will usually provide you with replacement income for a maximum of one year or until you have found alternate employment if sooner. You can add accident and sickness cover to this plan, which is known as ASU. However, I would always recommend income protection (above) as this is not yearly renewable so the insurance company cannot cancel on a whim! If you still require redundancy cover as well, run this separately

It is estimated that only one in eight of the working population have income protection even though it's such a big risk to take. You may feel you're invincible but having built up a decent living for yourself you will have far more to lose than you did before. If you're employed it may be that your employer will pay full wages for, say, four weeks and then a reduced amount for a further four weeks but then it comes down to the State and you could find a huge shortfall. If you are self-employed you are on your own and therefore it is even more of a priority!

Payment protection insurance
This is not to be confused with income protection mentioned above. I am totally unconvinced about this cover. It exists to pay your monthly loan payments should you fall ill or become unable to work for any reason. Why do I have reservations? Doesn't it sound like a good idea? It does until you read the small print and realize it doesn't cover the self-employed or those working on a contract. It's also very expensive and the cover it provides is generally quite limited to cover just one loan or credit card instead of your income.

Even worse than that is the fact that most people don't realize they are paying PPI on loans or credit card balances. When you take out a loan there is usually a 'with protection' or 'without protection' box to tick but often it's not pointed out by the salesperson. It is estimated that personal loan companies make at least £1 billion a year in commission on the back of 'selling' PPI to unsuspecting clients. PPI often slips by unnoticed on credit card statements and interest is charged on that as well as the original debt.

I would recommend rather than paying payment protection (PPI can add an average of 11 per cent to the monthly cost of a loan) that you take out an income protection policy with an insurance company. The pay-out will be far greater and you can choose what to do with the money rather than it being tied to the loan.

Now that we have looked at the different ways to protect yourself I hope you can see clearly that, although you will need to pay for the privilege of being covered, it's certainly money well spent. There's no point in making the climb if a knockback sends you right to the starting point or worse to behind where you were before we embarked on our financial adventure together.

STEP 20

NOT A PENNY MORE, NOT A PENNY LESS: PAY THE RIGHT AMOUNT OF TAX

*The art of taxation consists in so plucking the goose as to
obtain the largest possible amount of feathers
with the smallest possible amount of hissing.*
Jean Baptiste Colbert (Minister of Finance under Louis XIV)

Evading tax is illegal and therefore reckless and stupid. Tax planning is legal, sensible and strongly advised! Handing the taxman your hard-earned income by poor planning is not going to help you to achieve great wealth. Over two million people in the UK paid too much tax in 2007 either by not claiming the allowances available or by not supplying the Inland Revenue with up-to-date information. What an unnecessary waste of hard-earned cash and an extra barrier between you and your goal to become rich.

I know tax can be a minefield and the more affluent you become the more complex the situation can get but there are some important decisions you can make and steps you can take to stay on the right side of the law AND offset the impact of tax.

The intricacies of tax change so often but generally you should consider the following:

- Before you buy a product or service consider the tax situation wherever possible

- Certain investments have great tax breaks (ISAs, pensions). These should always be part of your financial planning

- Use all of your tax-free allowances – these are there to use so never lose out!

- Once you are able to afford the services of an accountant do so; a good accountant can end up saving you a small fortune

- If you are self-employed ask your accountant about establishing yourself as a limited company – this opens up an array of options not available to those who remain self-employed

- If you currently donate to charity or are considering it, do so by Gift Aid; the charity can then claim back basic-rate tax to increase the gift and if you are a higher rate taxpayer you can claim back 20 per cent of the donation. Now that's good news all round.

- If you are a non-taxpayer or if your taxable income is only slightly higher than your tax-free allowance (currently £6,035 for a single person under 65) you should complete form R85 and hand this to your bank or building society so you will not pay tax on your savings

- If you own shares, take advice on when to sell not only due to timing the markets but also so that you may use your

Capital Gains Tax allowance which is currently £9,600 per year

A great starting point is to check if you are paying the right amount of tax. The easiest way to do this if you're employed is to ask your employer to check your tax code. If you are self-employed ask your accountant to check for you. Most people who are paying too much tax could solve their situation with this little bit of homework.

You may have paid too much tax if:

- You have started a new job and had an emergency tax code for a while
- Your employer was using the wrong tax code
- You were only employed for part of the year
- You're a student who only worked over the holiday period and didn't complete the form P38S
- You had more than one job at the same time
- You had another income (normally taxed through your PAYE code) reduced. For example, where the Revenue had attempted to collect the tax due on savings or rental income via your PAYE code but the amount that had been included in the code was too high
- You stopped working and didn't get any taxable earnings or benefits for the rest of the year
- Your circumstances changed. For example, you retired, were made redundant or became self-employed

Next make sure that you are claiming all the allowances available to you. Everyone is entitled to a personal allowance, the amount you can earn before any tax is deducted; in 2008/2009 the allowance stands at £6,035. If you are married, make sure you both use your tax-free allowance fully by holding any savings in joint names or by transferring them to each other.

Many people lose out because they don't realize these allowances exist or that they are eligible. It is well worth checking whether you are eligible for working and child tax credit while you climb my steps. Obviously the higher you climb, the less you'll be able to claim and our aim is that you achieve your goal of wealth so ultimately you will certainly not be eligible. Make use of these schemes while you can.

By thinking ahead you can reduce your tax-bill significantly. So if you make a significant amount of money on the stock market later on in your climb, you can off-set this against any losses you have previously made. Many people don't realize that losses can be carried forward into the future. In terms of Capital Gains Tax, the current annual exemption as mentioned above is £9,200. If married, remember that assets can be transferred between spouses so that both exemptions can be used in full.

Let's now look at some of the main allowances you may be entitled to in the tax year 2008/2009.

Personal allowance
- Amount you can earn before paying tax per year: £6,035 (single person under 65); £9,030 (65–74) and £9,180 (75 and over)
- Married couple's allowance: £6,535 (aged under 75); £6,625 (75 and over)
- Blind person's allowance: £1,800 added to above allowances
- Payment on loss of office (if you are made redundant): £30,000 without paying tax
- Rent a room scheme: £4,250 is the amount you can receive without paying tax for income by renting a room in your house

It is so important to make sure your personal allowance is correct to make sure you are gaining from every opportunity given to you by the taxman!

Capital Gains Tax
- Annual exemption: £9,600. This is the amount you can make in profit without paying tax by a gain on, say, shares, selling a car or painting or any other item other than income earned by working

- All gains over the £9,600 are charged at 18 per cent tax rate

- Entrepreneurs' relief is for the selling of a business. The lifetime limit is one million pounds where tax is charged at a reduced rate of 10 per cent

My aim for you is to use these Capital Gains allowances because it will mean you have made enough money to start the process of buying and selling and making your very own gains!

Inheritance Tax
- We currently all have an exemption of £312k and now any unused amount if married or in a civil partnership can be carried forward to the surviving partner
- The tax rate charged on any excess amount over the exemption is a massive 40 per cent

Inheritance Tax (IHT) is to many the most cruel and unkind tax of all. We pay tax all our life and then again when we die or at least our beneficiaries do!

The very best way to deal with Inheritance Tax is to get

advice as soon as you have savings or property that would amount to anything like the nil rate band in order to plan ahead; trust and gifts can be used in order to mitigate Inheritance Tax. We will look at this in far more detail in Step 38, Pass Your Wealth on to Those You Love.

Of course, the taxation system has many more benefits and allowances but the information above contains the main allowances that affect us all every year. There are many other ways to save tax that are not as easy for the untrained eye to spot. Let's now look at a few of these less obvious tax breaks.

If you work from home, for example, you are entitled to claim a proportion of household expenses – heat, light and phone calls – against your income for the year. Even the taxman doesn't expect you to sit and freeze while trying to make a living working by candlelight! The proportion depends on the number of rooms used to run your business against the number of rooms in your house.

As already mentioned in Step 9, it makes sense for grand-parents to give children money to save as this will benefit from the child's own personal allowance. However, remember if the money comes from the parent the interest will be treated as taxable if it exceeds £100 per year. This is to stop parents simply holding larger sums in the child's name to avoid tax.

Of course, there are a number of investments available that you don't pay tax on like ISAs and premium bonds. Pensions have great tax breaks as well. If the idea of investigating the world of investments leaves you feeling less than enthusiastic go to a professional and get advice. It's worth paying for the best advice available. Staying one step ahead can save you a whole lot of cash. You don't want to give too much of the pie away to the Inland Revenue; use all of the tax breaks they allow . . .

It is important not to overlook **any** tax-saving opportunity (especially when times are tough) even if you think the savings will be negligible. It all adds up and the wealthier you become, the bigger these issues become. If at first you save enough on your tax bill to take out income protection or critical illness cover, you are doing yourself and your family one big favour.

Make sure you claim all you are entitled to and get advice from experts as you begin to create more wealth, since the more money you have, the more complex taxation becomes. And, as you climb further up the steps, the need to limit the amount of tax you pay becomes ever more important.

STEP 21

STEP ONTO THE PROPERTY LADDER

Empty pockets never held anyone back.
Only empty heads and empty hearts can do that.
Norman Vincent Peale

You've trusted me so far and now we're ready to make a big commitment: you *are* going to climb the property ladder. Whatever your struggle so far, put it behind you. No more wasted money on rent. We are going to make a big investment.

If you haven't yet made it onto the property ladder I will show you how it is possible. If you've been on the ladder but been knocked off or are struggling to make it on at all, don't worry. I can get you on the first rung. I will show you ways to make it onto the first rung that you'd maybe never considered before. And once you're on there I will show you, in the next step, how to get rich using property including buy to let, building your own home and building portfolios.

We all have little choice but to pay for the roof over our heads and so it makes sense to use the money we pay each month and make it an investment. Up to this point I have tried to drum home the madness of taking out loans and paying interest but the housing market is a unique exception. This is because over time (and hopefully not a very long time) the interest you pay each month on your mortgage will be less than the increase in the value of your property. Investing in assets like shares or property is the best way of beating inflation and building a tidy nest egg over the long term. 'Property is on the way down due to the credit crunch I hear you say.' However, the fact remains that over the *long* term both shares and property offer great potential.

There are some cases where renting is not a bad idea, when the market is at a peak and a slump is anticipated. By selling up and moving into rented accommodation temporarily, you 'bank' the profit you've made on your home when the market was buoyant. The trick is to buy back into the housing market when prices bottom out, maximizing your profit. But on the whole it is wiser to buy since money paid in rent will never be seen again and in some cases it is pricier to pay rent than to buy using a mortgage.

You can always increase your profits by moving to a property in a similar price range that may need repair work undertaken and therefore decreasing your mortgage for the next property and so on. This will inevitably save a fortune in interest payments but most people opt for a bigger and better house. This is also an investment and so either path will lead to greater wealth.

Yes, there will be fluctuations, peaks and troughs but you only have to look at what has happened in the property market over the last fifty years to see that property appreciates over time. Peaks and troughs are largely only relevant if you are forced to sell. Provided you allow yourself a comfortable margin to ensure that you can still meet repayments if interest rates soar, you are on a winning path.

By investing in property you set the base in a pyramid of

investment; this will guarantee you a secure future in terms of personal finance. The first and most important big investment you make should be in property. Once you have built the base you can move on to develop the rest of the building.

One of the most important things when getting on the first step of the property ladder is to examine your finances and ensure that you can afford the mortgage repayments (allowing for any future rises in interest rates). So many people who take on a low-start mortgage (this is where interest is deferred in the early years), drift for a couple of years making no plans for the sharp increase about to hit them. It is heartbreaking to lose your home, very stressful and can be avoided by not going beyond your means. If you would love to start off in a two-bed flat but can only be sure of covering the mortgage payments of a studio flat, then opt for the studio first. As you progress through the following steps you will be in a position to move into the home of your dreams but now is not the time to take unnecessary and potentially devastating risks.

In the UK we are a nation of housebuyers more than anywhere else in the world.

The fact that good old Britannia is a fairly small island means there is only so much space to go round. This compounds and escalates house prices. Most people dream of owning their own home. The UK Government recognizes that they need to assist people in buying their own home and have introduced a number of fantastic schemes that can help get you onto the property ladder. They are not in the media spotlight enough and many people do not know they even exist. I will share them with you now.

They are known as Affordable Home Ownership schemes:

New Build HomeBuy
Also known as Shared Ownership, this is a 'part buy part rent' scheme where you can purchase parts of the property and pay

rent on the unowned share to a registered social landlord (RSL). The rent is less than the mortgage payment, therefore saving you money. The great news is that any unowned share can be purchased at a later time when you are in a better financial position, and then the house is all yours! Properties are built specifically for New Build HomeBuy. Purchasing your first home this way will save you from overstretching yourself. The scheme is open to anyone who has a housing need and earns enough to keep up the monthly costs. All new-house builders in England need to set aside some of the new properties they build for New Build HomeBuy in order to obtain planning permission. These properties are then purchased by registered social landlords (RSLs) who then allow applicants to apply. You do *not* need any deposit to move forward as, even in the credit crunch we are now experiencing, you can obtain 100 per cent lending with this scheme

Open Market HomeBuy

Open Market HomeBuy is a low-cost Government-backed home-ownership programme. It is a flexible equity loan scheme designed to help households earning up to a maximum household income of £60,000 a year (subject to certain criteria) to buy either a second-hand home off the shelf via an estate agent or a brand-new home from a private developer. This programme is very popular and puts first-time buyers in particular (although it is also available to existing home owners in housing need) in the driving seat.

The product is designed specifically with the aim of helping local authority and housing association tenants, key workers and first-time buyers who are not able to afford to buy a suitable home in an area where they live or work on their own.

Key features of the Open Market HomeBuy programme include:

- Two different versions to consider: Ownhome and MyChoiceHomeBuy
- You can obtain an equity loan, which can be between 15 per cent and 50 per cent of the value of your property, to top up your own mortgage
- If you took up the Ownhome product, you would have a five-year interest-free period on the equity loan
- If you opted for MyChoiceHomeBuy, you would have the flexibility of obtaining your conventional mortgage from any qualified lender. Although the equity loan monthly charge starts sooner with MyChoiceHomeBuy, over time it may be a cheaper option

The products available

Ownhome and MyChoiceHomeBuy have been designed to suit a wide range of personal circumstances and you need to be aware of the various aspects of each in order to make an informed decision about which product best suits your needs.

Table 7 gives a simple overview of just some of their features.

How do I repay the equity loan?

VOLUNTARY REPAYMENTS
You can voluntarily repay the equity loan, in part or in full. You can do this as soon as your financial circumstances improve and not usually within the first year of ownership. Buying more shares is called 'Staircasing' and you can staircase out of the equity loan in 10 per cent chunks.

Table 7: Ownhome and MyChoiceHomeBuy main features

Ownhome	MyChoiceHomeBuy
Ownhome is provided by a partnership between Places for People (a housing association) and the Co-operative Bank and is part-funded by the Government. Places for People is an equity loan provider in its own right.	MyChoiceHomeBuy is part-funded by the Government and is offered by eight housing associations who form a funding and administrative consortium, each of which is an equity loan provider in its own right.
Key Facts	*Key Facts*
• Available throughout England	• Available throughout England
• You can borrow between 20% and 40% of the property price	• You can borrow between 15% and 50% of the property price, a little more generous than Ownhome
• If you qualified for a mortgage of £120,000, for example, you could buy a property worth up to £200,000, depending on your circumstances	• If you qualified for a mortgage of £120,000, for example, you could buy a property worth up to £240,000, depending on your circumstances
• You would need to get your conventional mortgage loan from the Co-operative Bank in the first instance; you cannot use any other lender so would need to be approved by them	• You would be able to obtain a conventional mortgage from any qualified lender; in principle, a good selection of high street lenders support this scheme
• You would not have to make any payments on the equity loan for the first five years	• You would pay a monthly interest charge on the loan based on 1.75% a year; this will rise with inflation each year
• After these five years, you would be charged at a fixed rate of 1.75% interest on the equity loan each year. After a further five years, this will increase to a fixed rate of 3.75%	
• You would not have to pay a deposit, though you could if you wanted to	• You would not have to pay a deposit, though you could if you wanted to

Compulsory repayments

You would have to repay the equity loan in full in the following circumstances:

- When the property is sold
- When your mortgage is finally paid off
- Upon the expiry of a default notice
- If you become insolvent
- When you no longer live in the property; in joint applications, this would be when the last of the original applicants was no longer resident

For further details about Open Market HomeBuy you need to contact your Regional HomeBuy Agent, a list of which can be seen on the Government's Housing Corporation website at www.housingcorp.gov.uk.

Welsh HomeBuy

The HomeBuy programme in Wales is operated and administered by housing associations. It is only available where the local authority decides that it is a priority for the use of their Social Housing Grant. It is targeted to help people buy their own homes who would otherwise require social rented housing.

Where the programme is available, the housing association will provide an equity loan for an agreed percentage (usually 30 per cent but up to 50 per cent in some areas) of the purchase price. The purchaser funds the balance through a conventional mortgage from a lender who supports the programme. Purchasers can also put in their own savings to boost their own purchaseability if savings are available.

There is no interest or monthly servicing fee on the equity loan; the equity loan is repaid as the same percentage of the value of the property at that time. The equity loan can be repaid at any time but must be repaid when the property is sold, as it is registered as a second charge behind the mortgage. For more information on Welsh

HomeBuy and how to apply for it, visit the Welsh Assembly at http://new.wales.gov.uk/ where information and a handy guide to the programme are available.

Scottish HomeBuy

The HomeBuy programme in Scotland is currently called Open Market Shared Equity Pilot and is almost identical in structure to the Welsh HomeBuy programme. It aims to help applicants on low to moderate household incomes who wish to become homeowners but cannot afford to pay the full price for a house. The programme is administered by the Scottish Government, with the exception of Edinburgh and Glasgow where it is administered by the respective city councils. For more information, visit www.scotland.gov.uk.

Northern Ireland HomeBuy

The programme in Northern Ireland is called Co-Ownership and is administered by the Northern Ireland Co-Ownership Housing Association Limited (which is better known as Co-Ownership Housing). Co-ownership is a 'Do It Yourself Shared Ownership' scheme (DIYSO) and operates broadly the same as the New Build HomeBuy programme in England whereby the applicant acquires a set share of a property by arranging a mortgage and perhaps putting down some savings as a deposit and also pays a subsidized rent on the share Co-Ownership Housing retains.

Having been available since the late 1970s, Co-Ownership has helped more than 19,000 households purchase the homes of their choice through shared ownership style assistance. Applicants take as large a share as they can afford to start with and can then increase that share at any time should their circumstances improve.

For the latest information on the funding available for this programme and the number of people who can be helped, visit www.co-ownership.org.

Social HomeBuy

This programme will provide new home ownership opportunities for existing social tenants (those tenants currently renting from a local authority or a housing association) who either don't have or can't afford the Right to Buy or Right to Acquire.

Basically a social tenant will be able to purchase a share in their current property and also benefit from a discount on the property's value. It can certainly be viewed as a half way house between Right to Buy and Shared Ownership. A minimum initial purchase share of 25 per cent applies and a nominal market rent will be charged on the share held by the local authority or housing association.

A select number of housing associations are assisting the programme from its launch in April 2006. To see if you are eligible, contact your social landlord for further information.

First-Time Buyers' Initiative
(incorporating the London Wide Initiative)

The First-Time Buyers' Initiative (FTBi) will certainly provide increased assistance to first-time buyers in their quest for affordable home ownership.

Although only launched in late 2006 this already very popular programme sees equity loans available (in a similar format to MyChoiceHomeBuy) to assist in the purchase of a newly built property. There are specific FTBi allocated properties available at specific sites nationwide which are within acknowledged regeneration areas. They are built by well known names such as Barratt Homes, Bellway, Crest

Nicholson and Taylor Wimpey. For more information about FTBi speak with your Regional HomeBuy Agent, details of which can be accessed from the Government's Housing Corporation website detailed above under the Open Market HomeBuy section.

All applicants need to be working people with only minor credit problems and minimum incomes in place depending on the area and nature of scheme. If you apply for one of the schemes you will need to be assessed by an expert IFA; visit www.bestadvice.co.uk for more information on what to do next.

Once you manage to get in on the ground level you'll never look back. Although there are some people who believe a mortgage is a millstone around the neck, mortgages only bring great stress if the people overstretch themselves and upset their whole financial balance and wellbeing. Go in at the right level and think carefully about what you can afford, anticipating future interest rates rises.

Eventually your mortgage will be far cheaper than the equivalent in rent, once inflation has done its work. You'll be sitting pretty in a place you can truly call your own and you will have made an investment for the long term. Now that's a solid base to build wealth on!

STEP 22

USE YOUR HOME TO MAKE MORE MONEY

I have been very poor the greatest part of my life, and have borne it
as well, I believe, as most people, but I can safely say that I have
been happier every guinea I have gained.
Sydney Smith

You are sitting *in* a gold-mine. Without realizing it, you eat, sleep
and watch television in your ticket to a richer future. Release the
potential hiding within your own four walls and start to play the
property game. I will show you ways to maximize your wealth
using your own home, in the shortest possible time.

How quickly you gain financial freedom from this step
depends on:

- The amount of money you have so far (you don't have to
  have any at this stage)
- Your ability to gain finance
- Your personal preferred level of risk

Winning is simply a matter of examining the possibilities

and deciding on the best options for you. There are numerous ways to make use of your principal residence to build wealth and I will show you the benefits of each:

- Rent a room – The Government has an approved Rent a Room scheme allowing you to rent a room in your house to a lodger without paying any tax on the first £4,250 received per annum. Tax credits aren't affected either so it's well worth considering if you have a spare room

- Register with film companies – You can make an absolute packet if your property is chosen as a film location and all you have to do is register, then sit back and hope to hear. Film companies are always on the lookout for new locations. Try registering with www.screenyorkshire.co.uk or www.greenwich.gov.uk/film/register.html. There are many others; carry out an online search.

- Bed and breakfast – Earn anything from £10–£50 per night per guest by offering a spare room in your house to bed and breakfast guests

And when you've created an income stream using your own home you may feel ready to enter the world of property management. This is where the big boys play and where serious money can be made. Five years from now you could be a property tycoon.

Until recent years making money out of property was seen as a preserve of the seriously rich or professional property developers. It definitely doesn't have to be that way; you can build a portfolio of property to guarantee you a secure and thriving income for the rest of your days. You do need to have money though to begin this step; if you do not have money, work on the earlier steps and save this step for later.

Buying to let can be a *real* money-spinner. The beauty of investing in the property market as a landlord is that you will receive a regular monthly income in the form of rent (at first this will only just about cover your costs, of course, but once inflation gets to work and rental yields increase, the mortgage payments will become easy to manage giving you an ever increasing surplus) plus your capital will be growing if the value of the property increases.

The first step to becoming a professional landlord is to raise some capital as an initial investment. But wait a minute, don't turn the page yet. It's really not as much as you think. You *can* build a property portfolio. Read on, I will show you how.

Firstly you need to appreciate that this step needs to be seen as a long-term investment to take market fluctuations into account. The last thing we want to happen is a fall in the market with you as the unfortunate fellow left holding the last 'hot potato'. . . However, due to the credit crunch, there are going to be so many good opportunities out there for you!

So provided that you're in a position to sit it out for the long term I think you're on to a winner if you go ahead and become a property investor. Ideally you would have a 20 per cent deposit to put down on your first property, perhaps by re-mortgaging on your main residence or using savings (if you have any).

If you live in a very expensive area don't be disheartened, you can buy anywhere. Although I would advise purchasing in the UK to start with. Choose an area where prices are cheaper. Buying close to a station or university is always great for letting quickly and prices seem to hold there if other prices become unstable.

Once you have enough equity built up in one property you can access it via re-mortgaging and thereby create a deposit to buy another property.

As each property you invest in gains equity (simply a

waiting game) you can re-mortgage to release the funds and repeat the process, gradually building your own property portfolio. Also by following the previous steps you should be building extra capital by now; if you like the idea of property investment use the deposit needed as your goal!

You could try buying at auction to maximize profits. There are definitely bargains to be had but the downside is that you have to be ready to move quickly (usually within one month) or you could lose your deposit. If you have nerves of steel and faith in your solicitor to complete on time, then register with several auction houses and have a browse through their prospectus.

Another way to make a large profit in a short amount of time is to build your own house. There is little doubt that, if carefully managed and realistically thought out, building your own home can make a vast amount of money in a reasonably short space of time. Even Ikea now offer flat pack houses! £100k for a one-bedroom property. But there are a number of pitfalls to avoid and strategies to put in place before embarking on a mission like this.

And, finally, it is possible to make money out of other people's property as well as your own. You can register with a house sitting agency and travel the country staying in some of the nicest homes and get paid for the pleasure. If you're self-employed and your work is mobile it can make the perfect combination. The bonus is that you get paid for the pleasure, normally about £20–£25 per day. Check out www.housesitter sltd.co.uk.

STEP 23

PLAN FOR YOUR RETIREMENT

Time is more value than money.
You can get more money but you cannot get more time.
Jim Rohn

As the old Chinese proverb goes, with money you can buy an expensive clock but you can't buy time. And that's true to a certain extent but what you can buy is free time – time away from the hamster wheel most people find themselves in. And you can buy yourself an easy retirement.

There are a whole host of reasons why you should make it a priority to put money aside for when you're older and the number one reason is that the State cannot provide for your old age as they have in the past. The Department for Work and Pensions is encouraging people of all ages to join the safety net of providing for when they no longer work and I am 100 per cent behind this message. With more people retiring than ever, the Government will not be able to afford the rising costs. It's simple maths and is not a party political issue (or should not be).

The state pension is inadequate and will not be an option to rely on in the twenty-first century. A supplement to the state pension is not a luxury but a necessity if you want to maintain a reasonable standard of living into old age.

I'm not suggesting you give up work altogether, not at all. I don't intend to EVER. I love working and love what I do. And looking at the statistics for men at retirement will be enough to keep me plugging away into my old age; it seems that lots of men pop off very soon after receiving the golden handshake. If you work for 40 or 50 years and then stop, it must feel like you're staring into a void. And, as for having no money, retirement is no more than a living death sentence. Much better to keep your finger in a number of different pies. Even though your plan should be to build income streams to make you rich, you still need to build a pension because it is income you can rely on. And it's the very best route to buying yourself time that I can think of for your future

It's wonderful to think that you can buy yourself some time for days in your future. We've already established that it may be a little optimistic to think that you can buy happiness and you certainly can't buy good health but you can buy yourself time.

Time is the one thing that most people are short of. Many people spend a large part of their life in dead-end jobs that they are tied to through financial commitments. Building financial security allows you the luxury of buying some time off to do things you have perhaps always dreamed of.

Bearing in mind that life expectancy is increasing at the rate of three years for every ten years that passes, there is an awful lot of time between your last day of work and your last day on the earth. I should re-phase that – I'm not suggesting it's awful, of course not! It's most definitely a good thing. It gives you a whole lot more time to enjoy the wealth you are in the process of amassing. It does mean though that if you want to remain in the lap of luxury for the rest of your days, then it's wise to make plans for that time well in advance. Do something about it now!

I know many people who are so busy dealing with the priorities of today and tomorrow that they put off retirement plans as something to worry about in the future. They plan for mortgage payments and food bills, Christmas, holidays, car tax, etc. Everything goes on their list except one of the most important investments you can ever make. Time just slips away.

Join me for a little team-talk:

- Move pension provision to the top of your *need* list; scrub out that weekend in the Lake District (do that next year)

- A pension is the very best way of providing a replacement income for old age. Consider making an effort to catch up on lost years by injecting an initial lump sum into your retirement plan

- Making the transition from a working life to one dependent on savings is not always easy. Knowing you have built a very comfortable nest egg will smooth the path rather nicely

- Don't delay any longer. The second level of your financial pyramid is beckoning. Build before it's too late

Once an annuity (income) is purchased from the pension pot you have built up, you can opt for the payments to continue until you die or even have the payments guaranteed for the lifetime of both you and your spouse or guaranteed for say five or ten years in any event. Many pension companies do not explain the many ways payments can be taken and I believe this will be the next mis-selling scandal; therefore please make sure you take independent financial advice (IFA) before choosing any option as once taken there is no changing your mind!

In a strange way pension income is safer than your regular salary since you can always lose your job or get made redundant but with pension income you are in control. In addition it has a major tax advantage:

- You can withdraw up to a 25 per cent tax-free lump sum from your fund at retirement

Furthermore, while saving for retirement:

- Contributions paid in towards your pension attract tax relief at your highest rate payable

- The fund grows free from Capital Gains Tax

These tax concessions allow the fund to grow faster than other savings.

Personal pensions can be drawn any time after the age of 55 and you can even keep working full time. So if you've left pension provision on the back burner and time is ticking away, it may be wise to make a lump-sum investment into a pension fund to catch up if you can.

In later years it's not unusual to find you're in a larger house than you need. It can then sometimes make sense to downsize, thereby saving on mortgage interest payments, fuel bills, and council tax, etc. The saving will make an excellent injection into your pension fund.

If you are employed and you can join an occupational scheme, then that is a must. You will benefit from the fact that your employer will have usually negotiated lower charges and often will make a contribution for you into your pension pot.

Never take out a private pension instead of joining an occupational scheme.

If your employer does not offer a pension scheme or you are self-employed, then seek independent financial advice for the very best pension for you. Remember: the longer you wait, the more it will cost. Be smart, think ahead.

PART THREE

BUILDING ON WEALTH

STEP 24

BECOME RICH BY SERVING THE MEGA-RICH

If you can actually count your money, you are not really a rich man.
John Paul Getty

'You rang m'lud?' Did you know that it's possible to become rich by serving the mega-rich? It may be surprising but there are more domestic staff being employed these days than at any other time including the Victorian era. And the salaries and experience of such staff compare very little to those we associate with the old 'upstairs, downstairs' days.

Modern butlers command salaries of £100k+ and many jet set all over the world with their employers who can be anyone from celebrities to corporate CEOs, city whiz-kids or media tycoons.

Being a rich man's servant is a pretty good racket to get into these days and can lead to a prosperous lifestyle for the 'lowly' servant. Many people who find themselves in a position of having 'new money' have no idea how to behave in their new arena, and the services of someone experienced who can guide them is of immense value to them.

Hedgefunders, private equity kings and venture capitalists can become super-rich almost overnight and need a guiding hand to help them cope with their instant wealth and get them a table at the restaurant of their choice.

Of course, being a butler is only one of many ways of serving the super-rich. There are many services the rich will pay through the nose for and there are spiralling numbers of very rich people in the world. Did you know, for example, that half of America's total personal wealth has been created in the last ten years? When you figure the record number of new millionaires making an entrance in countries such as China, Russia and India you realize the astounding levels of new wealth throughout the entire world, not just in Western society.

The number of mega-homes all over the world has spiralled in recent years and owners need thoroughly modern male or female servants who can manage vast estates and be the ultimate problem solvers.

Time to capitalize on the situation! If you have something to sell to these people, get it out there on the market. Never has there been a hotter time to cash in. Take the waiting list for Ferraris for example – if you want one you have to get in the queue and wait for over a year. If you want a Gulfstream 500 you'll have a three- or four-year wait. If a yacht is what you're hoping to buy when you make it rich, perhaps you should get your order in now as the wait for one of these little beauties can be up to five years because makers are regularly inundated with orders. All you have to do is come up with something the rich will lust after, or even just cater for their basic needs. This will bring home the money.

It is worth mentioning here, just out of interest – there are a number of hookers who make a fabulous fortune from servicing the rich. And there are an awful lot of rich men who are more than willing to give a fair portion of their copious wealth to a girl who can give him exactly what he wants, when he wants it. Come to mention it, one of my very successful female clients, cash rich, time poor, uses the services of gigolos. She works 16 hours a day, has little time to fraternize with men and often those she comes across in business are threatened by her power (not sure why; I find it exciting!). But she still needs some attention and affection in her time off. It revitalizes her, gives her energy, makes her feel connected to the world, and I am led to believe that the men she 'uses' are very well rewarded. I'm certainly not suggesting that this is the way to go, but it's an interesting example of how the abounding wealth of the super-rich can trickle down to the ordinary man/woman on the street.

The great bonus in catering to the whims of the mega-rich is that they have the money to pay for anything they want. Salaries for nannies, PAs, private chefs, chauffeurs, etc are rising all the time, basically because they can afford to pay.

A number of websites have recently materialized to capitalize on the willingness of some to enjoy the profits of other people's hard work (or perhaps their inherited fortunes). There is a new breed on the loose in today's society and they're out to get all they can. They enjoy nothing more than designer clothes, expensive food and all the trappings of a rich existence. Enter the sugar daddy (or mummy). Youth and beauty have always been valued and those that possess it can command a lavish lifestyle without having to lift a finger.

Marrying into wealth has many benefits and, after all, what these treasure seekers are left with is a absolute fortune. Membership of websites like www.sugardaddie.com or www.seekingmillionaire.com are growing at a staggering 4,000 every week and two-thirds of the members are women. In exchange for their youth and beauty they get an average of £7,000 a month expenses and are often set up in their own flat. Don't knock it until you try it!

But wait a minute, building your wealth on other people's fortunes – isn't that a bit like building a house upon the sand? Is it all about to come to an end in one big crash? I don't think so, not a bit of it. The new wealth we see is being fuelled by new technology such as the internet and personal electronics combined with a huge increase in financial speculation (global stocks and shares, buyouts, property investors, etc) just as the advent of radio and cinema, cars and telephones created a boom in the roaring twenties. In *Wealth and Democracy*, the author Kevin Phillips believes that, 'in an age of excess, technology and finance joined to lead the way.'

Yes, there is certainly a huge river of money that flows throughout the world today, from London to New York and through China and Russia – places no one would have dreamed of as being wealthy ten or fifteen years ago. It is amazing to realize that China alone holds more than $1.7 trillion savings deposits. I think the boom is here to stay for a long while yet. Obviously there will be natural peaks and troughs along the way but the river will keep on flowing – we just have to entice you to the edge, to dip your toes in and then swim with the tide.

The spending habits of the ultra-rich will continue to help drive the global economy, and any business that caters to this growing class will be unlikely to fail. Adapting to the changes in the economy is the key to future prosperity. If you can think of a luxury that the rich will lust after, aim to get it out there quickly – the queue for your service will continue to grow more quickly than you can meet its demand.

STEP 25

DON'T ACCEPT EVERYTHING YOU'RE TOLD

I am a millionaire. That is my religion.
George Bernard Shaw, Major Barbara

Before you take advice take responsibility. This book will give you all the information you need to reach your richer future but along the way you will need to work with an independent financial adviser to take advice about purchasing your stocks/shares/investments. And you will need to use the services of estate agents and perhaps lettings agents when making property decisions.

Professional advisers have their place, of course. They can be useful, particularly where your knowledge in certain areas lets you down. If you intend to go it alone, there's an awful lot of information to digest, most of it in jargon used only by advisers in that field. Asking for help to decipher 'financial or legal terms' is of course well advised but make sure that you are clear on the cost and you understand how the adviser works.

Here are my tips for choosing an adviser to work with:

- Always, but always, take independent financial advice (IFA). Some advisers are tied to one company. This means they are salespeople for that company whereas an 'IFA' works on your behalf to find *you* the best deal

- Meet with two or three advisers and compare them before deciding who to work with. Tell them you intend doing this before meeting with them!

- Make sure you feel comfortable in their presence and you could ask any question you may have without feeling apprehensive

- Ask them how long they have held their current position. If they jump from company to company it is unlikely they would be there for you over the long term. (This is important when dealing with your finance and helps to build trust.)

- Ask them to tell you about their experience and check if they are registered with the FSA by visiting their website www.fsa.gov.uk

- Ask if they are happy for you to seek references from any already happy and satisfied clients (all good advisers should not have any problem with this)

- Ask about their charges, if they work for a fee or by commission

- Trust your own instincts!

So let's make a start to find you the best adviser to work with you. Visit www.unbiased.co.uk. This site allows you to search for an adviser close to your home or place of work and even choose your adviser by gender or area of expertise. It also explains and assesses the different quualifications that advisers may have. Furthermore I was asked to film a podcast on this site to explain how to find a good adviser and what you can expect when working with an IFA. So when you visit, search 'Paul Banfield' to follow my advice.

I believe even if you take advice that it's still always best to listen to your inner voice. You know the sensible one you don't always want to hear. If something doesn't feel right, just don't do it. If you are going to invest money you need to have faith in the person you are to work with.

It is possible, however, on many occasions to be your own adviser. Think of all the questions you need to ask and then try to answer them yourself using your new-found knowledge and common sense. You will become more confident every step of the way. Take advice when you feel you need too; that way you'll have the best of both worlds!

If you are investing in a business venture you have to judge both the venture and the people to be involved in the project and if there are any little warning bells, however faint, listen to them and walk away. We've all had times where we know something isn't quite right. We've had a gut feeling but have ignored it, perhaps to our peril. If you are so keen to plough ahead with your plans that you choose to ignore your inner voice, you will regret it. When the plan involves your livelihood, it's crucial that you trust your intuition.

Never do any business with anyone you do not trust. If you had no trust in your bank you would withdraw your money (as we witnessed hoards of Northern Rock customers doing in the autumn of 2007). Strong logic and due diligence are paramount priority but also trust your instincts. Take advice sure, but rely on no one but yourself to make any final decision.

There are an awful lot of people ready and willing to give you financial advice – as mentioned make sure they're independent. If they're restricted to advising on a product range which is limited by the company they work for, then the advice they give cannot possibly be impartial. The danger is that you could end up with products that pay the highest commission and your needs may come a very poor second. It's a bit like shopping for a car. If you go to a franchise selling only a particular brand, you will end up with that make of car for sure. It may be good, it may be bad. However if there were a garage that sold every make of new car available in the UK, after good advice you would expect to leave with the very best!

STEP 26

BEWARE OF MAKING *FAST* MONEY

He that diggeth a pit shall fall into it.
Ecclesiastes 10:8

Making money requires time, dedication and hard work; there's no way round it, over it or under it. Read my lips, there is NO quick fix. Please acknowledge this fact early on in your quest so that you don't get sidetracked or tempted by dodgy swindles designed by fraudsters (down-right criminals in other words). Being over-anxious to get rich quick can lead to unwise decision making and ultimately therefore disappointment.

Having said all that, there are some quick and easy ways to make money and in the next step I will reveal them to you. I'm not talking about the 'get rich quick' cons you find plastered all over the place, from shop windows to street signs. The 'ring this number and I will give you a part-time job working from home on a 60k salary with company car thrown in'. These kinds of schemes do make fast money but only for the con-artists who dreamed them up in the first place. It's a pretty low method of creating wealth, particularly since most of the applicants will be young mums or perhaps disabled people in need of a home-based income.

Always be very wary of anyone who offers to get you rich quick. These schemes prey on the eagerness of people to become wealthy with the minimum effort. It is sad because it almost always ends in tears.

I remember reading about an international cheque scam recently where the fraudsters made contact with people who were advertising goods or services for sale, perhaps in a free paper, on the internet or by way of a card in a shop window. The scammers managed to con large numbers of people out of thousands of pounds by posing as genuine buyers of the goods and then paying for them using counterfeit cheques.

It works like this. Initially the seller is contacted by the fraudster, usually by email or via a mobile telephone call, who offers a cheque for an amount substantially higher than the price of the goods or service. The seller is then asked to transfer the excess amount from his or her own funds, and is sometimes even offered a cash incentive to do so. This sort of scam works so well because it is playing on people's greed.

I know, I know, you're thinking that anyone who falls for a hoax like this must have lost his mind but it's so often switched-on people in search of a better future who fall victim. So just to get it straight in your own mind: no one, repeat, no one is going to get you rich quick. If you work closely alongside me and stick to the principles explained in each step you will achieve wealth but it won't happen overnight (except by a lottery win or a rich auntie, if you have one).

In our electronic age it's even easier for fraudsters to pull the wool over unsuspecting eyes. You don't have to be a fool to fall prey to deception, it happens all too easily. Knowing what to look out for can help you to avoid becoming a victim.

It is difficult to provide an exhaustive list of scams and

swindles since there are so many variations, many involving the internet, but what follows is a summary of the ones I've been told of by those unfortunate enough to have been scuppered:

- Stolen Identity Fraud – Identity fraud is on the increase. Criminals are now managing to obtain personal information with ease and get their hands on money you think is safe. Keep a close eye on your credit card and bank statements or you could find you're accumulating debts that aren't even yours. Fraudsters may even raid your bin to obtain your financial details. Shred all letters, bills and receipts before discarding and stay one step ahead of them

- Accessing Secure Information – Beware of anyone getting hold of your bank details by way of hacking into your computer or dirty telephone tricks. If you receive an email from someone you don't know, delete it. Don't let curiosity get the better of you. Hackers plant viruses in spam emails and can access all your personal information that way. Similarly fraudsters try to gain PIN or security numbers from you by pretending to be your friendly bank, via telephone or email. A genuine caller from your bank would never ask for these details

- The automatic teller machines (ATM) – hole in the wall – are being hit big time as fake slots, placed inside the original slot, read our cards and a small camera is placed above in order to read the numbers we tap onto the key pad. Shield the keypad using your spare hand in order to stop this dastardly scam

- Phishing – These fraudsters are also after your personal information and bank details. They try to obtain these by setting up a fake internet site that closely resembles the genuine article. They often go for bank or government institutions. One of my clients experienced one of these sites when he advertised some goods on eBay and received a reply from a 'customer' who claimed to have paid for the goods. The 'customer' sent an email in a format very similar to the official site but luckily my client kept his eyes open and spotted the con immediately

• Pharming – This goes one step further. Con artists have now found a way of forwarding their fake website on to you as soon as you attempt to access your online bank account. Beat the bogus con artists by updating your virus software regularly

• Chain letters – Chain letters work (if that's the right word) by persuading the victim to send a copy of the letter to several new recipients, and to send something else (usually money) to the people named in the letter. By adding their names to the bottom of the list, victims hope eventually to get some money back from other people further down the chain. This is usually a forlorn hope but so many people get drawn in by the promise offered by these letters, sometimes attracted by the possibility of getting rich quick or otherwise through fear of repercussions if the instructions are not adhered to. This is especially true with the elderly. That's what makes this scandal so outrageous. The classic 'make money fast' letter consists of several sections with the general suggestion that all your dreams will come true if you simply forward the letter on to as many people as possible. It will often contain testimonials from others who have been successful

• Pyramid Schemes – These schemes get their name because money works its way to the top of the 'pyramid' and it's only the people at the top who gain any benefit. The scheme only works if the supply of new recruits signing up continues endlessly. Trouble is that the supply inevitably dries up and those halfway up the pyramid lose everything

- Share Scams – If you get a telephone call from a perfect stranger who tries to persuade you to buy shares in a company you've never heard of, let those warning bells tinkle. In fact let the bell ring loudly, 'Leave well alone!'

- Internet Auction Sites – These sites are not always all they appear to be. There are fantastic sites available that have enabled many people to create an extra income stream but, sadly, there are all too many people who have been conned out of their money as the goods are never sent. Only buy from high feedback sellers

Of course I won't add gambling to the list since it involves choice, but I'm tempted to since it is about as far away as you can get from the strategy of wealth building. The thing to remember about gambling is that the house always has the edge over the punter. Whether it's the bookies or the casino, they will always have the advantage or they wouldn't stay in business (and remember they do business very well indeed). The advantage they have is often referred to as the 'House Edge'.

On the roulette wheel for example, bets on the layout carry a 2.7 per cent edge in favour of the house. For those who like to dabble on the poker table, they are playing against a 2 per cent edge for the house. Blackjack with six decks carries a house edge of 0.55 per cent, if the player was playing to perfection.

Of course, all the above figures are the average expectations but can vary due to individual customer playing styles.

There are many books and websites designed to 'help' you devise your best playing strategy, but my advice is always to visit a casino expecting to lose money.

But come on, you already knew that didn't you? You wouldn't expect to see a visit to 'the dogs' featured in my strategy of 'How a Build a Portfolio', would you?

I mention dog racing because it is an interesting form of gambling since there are strategies you can employ that will allow you to come out on top if you had enough money to keep betting. In a dog race you would normally see six dogs racing. Therefore if you always bet on the same trap (let's say trap 1) the law of averages would suggest you'll have a winning bet 1/6 (16.6 per cent) of the time.

So it is only the odds that make this unacceptable. If you were always able to place enough money every time in every race in order to recoup previous lost money and a profit if your chosen track 1 did win, this would bring logic to gambling and would (if you did not miss a race) build a return, because you are not relying on chance i.e. one dog being faster than the other. Pure luck or 'form' would not play a part because of logic (even the skulduggery would even out in the track that you have chosen).

But I'm not for one second suggesting that you head off for Wimbledon with all the spare cash you can muster crammed into the deep pockets of your Arthur Daley overcoat. Gambling is grease on the rungs of the ladder you've just hauled yourself up and one of the fastest routes to poverty to be found. The scams outlined earlier will cause a dent to appear in your accumulated wealth but hopefully once bitten twice shy. With gambling, once bitten it has you by the teeth and it may be hard for you to let go. Best don't go there in the first place.

A new area of gambling that many people now find interesting is spreadbetting. Spreadbetting offers an exciting challenge to seasoned market players. Instead of buying shares, the spreadbetter places a bet that a certain company's share price will either go up or down. The more the share moves, the greater the payout.

There are tax advantages for the spectator who holds a large portfolio. The disadvantage is the risk factor, but that's exactly why it draws in the thrill seeking crowds.

I hope these examples (and there are many I haven't mentioned) have shocked you into realizing that making fast money walks hand in hand with losing money fast. Make this one of your personal mantras and let's get on with the job of making you rich.

STEP 27

USE SECRET
MONEY-MAKING TIPS

Understand this, I mean to arrive at the truth. The truth, however
ugly in itself, is always curious and beautiful to seekers after it.
Hercule Poirot

The secret to making money is that there are no secrets, just
good clear thinking and hard work! Were you anticipating
quick and easy solutions to the worldwide problem of
poverty? Well, if there are any I've never come across them.
I've known a few financial surprises in my time but, alas, no
secrets.

And do you really want secrets anyway? I'm not a big fan
of them myself. That's partly why I'm writing this book – I
want to share my knowledge, not keep it sneakily hidden
away like some special breed of financial freemason. I believe
that to become wealthy you need dogged determination and
you need to sweat blood and tears. That's all I know and it's
no secret. Oh and there are pacts with the devil but I never
stooped to that myself.

No, I don't think there are any secrets that will propel you into mega-wealth but don't be disheartened. There are a few insider tips that are not generally very well-known outside of the financial arena and I'm happy to share these with you.

But please pay heed to my word of warning – don't go buying secret ways of making money from anyone. The writers of expensive newsletters promising copious amounts of cash from 'sure-fire' stock market investments are banking on the 'there's one born every minute' theory. Become wise to them. They don't know any special secrets any more than you do. I think it's good to dispel the money myths. Becoming aware of money and the pitfalls will help to move you in the right direction.

Having said all that, the right information is invaluable. I have spent the last twenty-two years building a bank of experience in wealth building. I have learnt ways to get there faster and with much less effort. With my knowledge and tips it would only take me ten now, if I had to start over.

For instance, now I take advantage of the forty days in a year where investments make up to 80 per cent of their money. Learning when to be in or out is an art and perfecting the art makes the real money.

This is one of the closely guarded secrets of the financial world but why keep it secret? I want you to use it to your advantage as I have. Invest money in unit and investment trusts around October as fund managers are rewarded bonuses on their performance at the end of the year; it's in their interest for our investments to do well in the last quarter, they will pull out all the stops!

When directors buy, it is wise to buy; and when they sell, you do the same. The thing is that company directors know when a good thing is about to happen. They know if there are bad times ahead. They are the insiders; they know when there's an issue (good or bad) because they're right there in the boardroom. I believe director dealings are the best indicator of market performance that amateur share dealers can lay their hands on. Watch what they get up to and the crucial times to act, use the share dealing sites and national newspapers to look at directors' meetings as it's compulsory that these purchases are disclosed – this is called directors' dealings.

Of course, directors are fallible too and many studies have been conducted claiming that there is no connection between what the directors do and their company's share price but I have little doubt that when a director starts to sell large chunks of the shares he owns, it's a pretty good sign that you should do the same. You only have to examine what happened shortly before the 'technology bubble' burst in 2000 and again just before the bank shares went into freefall in 2008. That's right, you guessed it: many of them got out in time . . .

In the financial world, to make money fast, you either need to find a niche in the market or time the market correctly. As in all business deals in life, buying and selling at the correct time is crucial.

As Zachary Scott would have it, 'As you grow older, you'll find the only things you regret are the things you didn't do.' The secret of making a fortune is recognizing when the time is right to be in and when to be out.

There are a number of investment strategies that take advantage of market volatility and they are an excellent way of maximizing purchasing power. You can invest fixed amounts at regular intervals into an investment to build a portfolio of stocks and shares and benefit from the natural price fluctuations that occur in the market by benefiting from pound cost averaging. We look at this in more detail in Step 32.

Investing directly in shares in some sectors can be extremely rewarding; often there are signs to look out for. Take, for example, when the developed world decreases, the emerging markets usually perform well. Early in the new year the leisure industry does very well as everyone clambers to the gym trying to wear off some of the Christmas turkey and treats.

Most people don't realize that there is an opposite correlation between interest rates for mortgages and deposit accounts. When interest rates become more expensive, investors receive a better return and vice versa – the 'Yin and Yang' effect. The average always works in favour of the investor though. Make use of this knowledge and make it work for you.

STEP 28

BRING OUT THE BIG GUNS

I can assure you, mademoiselle, that where money is concerned I am strictly a man of business.
Hercule Poirot

'Wait a minute' I can hear you moan, 'We know what we're not supposed to do if we want to get rich. We mustn't pay too much tax (or too little), mustn't spend more than we earn, we know we won't get rich quick on the back of someone else's schemes and we mustn't believe everything we're told just because we see a pin-stripe suit. We know all the things we can't do – so what can we do?!'

The answer is that you must take a few minutes to congratulate yourself. You have made a small investment, made steps to joining the property ladder and made provision for your retirement in the form of a pension. Pat yourself on the back, then take a deep breath and gather all your wits about you as we are now moving together to join the big boys.

This is where you'll need to draw on the confidence we discussed in the earlier steps. It's time to bring out the big guns!

We've climbed a long way now and hopefully you've managed to stash a few important lessons under your belt and a fair bit of cash away in various 'baskets'. I now want you to walk with me into the colourful world of investments. You have to play smart to keep ahead of the game when it comes to investing large sums of money.

But before we bring out the ammo I want to repeat one of my most used catchphrases. The one involving eggs and a basket, it really is one motto that has seen so many people through difficult times and done them proud.

Ignore it and you may still prosper but there's a more than reasonable chance that you'll fluff it big time and meet with disaster. There are people who have obtained fantastic returns while squirreling all of their eggs in one basket but they stand the chance of losing their money as quickly as it has been gained. The key is to work out a strategy before jumping in with both feet and always, always spread the risk.

Building a portfolio of investments is an ideal way to do this because the world of finance is one big circle: 'what goes around comes around'. Spreading your money across sectors, investments and opportunities spreads the risks. It's a bit like building a house: a good foundation is required but you must have the correct shape and size bricks. The cement that holds the house together is the information and knowledge – this I will share with you.

Bonds and fixed interest securities are one of the most popular investments for people who have built a sum of money and are an ideal base for the bottom of the pyramid we are about to build. In the next few steps we'll explore other investments that involve perhaps a little more risk.

In simple terms, a bond is a tradable written guarantee on the part of the issuer to fulfil a number of obligations relating to the payment of dividends/growth or interest and the repayment of capital. There can also be options attached to the bond allowing them to be converted into something else but this is not always the case.

They are tradable because they can be sold, thereby converting them into cash. But they can be kept until their maturity date. It may be that the only evidence you have of purchasing a bond is an account entry or you may receive a document confirming you as the owner.

Prices go up and down constantly depending on which type of bond you hold and are affected by:

- Current and projected inflation rates
- Current and projected market interest rates
- Economic 'good' or 'bad' news
- The potential for further bond issues
- The price of the shares or other assets held within the bond

As with all investments, staying power is the biggest factor in success. If you decide to cash in the bond before it matures, you may get less money back than your original investment as a result of a penalty or fluctuations in the market.

Of course, government bonds offer the most secure investments. They are known as 'gilt-edged' securities because it is highly unlikely that the capital will not be repaid. In over 100 years of bond issues the Government has never failed to pay capital or interest due.

Leading bonds in today's market are:

- UK government bonds – A dominating leader in the market of bonds offering a benchmark to all other bonds issued. The return is usually lower than with other bonds but this is traded against the security that comes with a government bond

- Index-linked gilts – The dividend payments of this type of bond and the capital are linked to inflation, based on the

Retail Price Index. You are consequently almost guaranteed a real return if you hold until maturity. The downside is that they are harder to sell in the market than conventional gilts and so are less liquid

- Undated gilts – The most widely known undated gilt is the War Loan, the oldest of all gilts dating back to the seventeenth century. They have no specific redemption date but can be redeemed by the Government if they chose to

- Supranational bonds – These are issued by the World Bank or European Investment Bank and are almost as secure as government bonds, paying interest just once instead of the usual twice a year

- Corporate bonds – Issued by companies, they work in the same way as government and supranational bonds but they have a higher risk and so tend to offer a higher yield

- High yield bonds – The possibility of default on one of these bonds is high and so, as expected, they yield a high return. If you want to go for this level of danger, it's a good idea to spread the risk

- Overseas bonds – Almost every country in the world offers government and corporate bonds. While it may appear that overseas bonds offer a high yield, bear in mind that if there is a sudden movement in exchange rates the return on your investment could be destroyed

- Insurance company bonds are a different type of vehicle available both on and off shore (bond funds). They allow you to invest in funds via the umbrella of the wrapper and they have certain tax advantages

Points to remember:

- Deviation, not putting your eggs in one basket is my catch-phrase. Financial advisers call this 'spreading the risk'

- When building a portfolio it is important to remember that the more adventurous you are, the greater chances you have of making more money; conversely, you give yourself the greatest chance of losing money. (This is where timing the markets comes in, i.e. buying and selling at the right time.)

- Make sure you build a firm foundation; this allows you to build a strong financial house that will not be blown away

- Keep up to date with all your investments in order for you to know if you need to make any changes at any point

- Always take independent financial advice when you feel out of your comfort zone or to help you on your way!

STEP 29

INVEST IN ALL THAT GLITTERS . . .

There stands a lady on a mountain, who she is I do not know,
All she wants is gold and silver; I shall to the mountain go!
Anon, Kiss in the Ring

The world of investments is about to get even more colourful and a little bit sparkly too. Invest in precious metals and it's likely that the rest of the steps you climb will be paved with gold. Jump on the golden bandwagon and you'll be on your way to a glittering future. All you have to do is buy your way to wealth by investing in precious metals. Gold has a long history of being the most precious metal on earth and has been used as a form of money for thousands of years. Since the beginning of civilization gold has formed the bedrock of value, measured by the 'gold standard'.

Gold was once seen as the territory of cranks and eccentrics and many people have lost their lives in the clamour for it. People have always travelled around from place to place, bartering the goods they own for the things they need for survival, risking attacks from bandits along the way. The promise of gold has long since been a potent motivator to travel. Gold has been worshipped since early civilization and the lust for it has increased through the ages.

Ironically, the more it was lusted after, the less there seemed to be. Its scarcity created a vicious circle; when someone managed to get their hands on some they clung to it for dear life and so it remained out of circulation for a long time. At one point the short supply of gold led a European church to melt down its crucifix. The addiction to gold throughout Europe increased through the centuries and the wealthy clamoured for it. They couldn't get enough of it in their houses, furniture, and all their possessions.

Conversely, in the gold-rich land of the Sudan, gold miners would do anything to get their hands on the commodity they were short of – salt. Miners sweated profusely and without their own salt deposits they struggled for survival. Salt was so valuable in the region that it could be exchanged for an equal amount of gold with traders from the West. Cubes of salt were used as both food and money in Africa. (The word salary comes from the Latin word *sal*, meaning salt.)

Europeans travelled to the Sudan in a quest for gold, hunting for the mines that concealed the stuff of their dreams but the Sudanese tried to keep the origins of their gold secret and tried to convince travellers from the West that gold grew in the ground as carrots do and it was the ants that brought it to the surface. They were well aware that the lust for gold would lead some to be willing to commit murder. The innate lust for gold was used by one young Roman emperor as a source of amusement; he would toss gold coins from the top of a basilica and get a thrill from watching the citizens below fight to the death to get hold of some. No wonder Shakespeare described gold as, 'poison to men's souls'.

Treasure seekers throughout the ages have been willing to dice with danger for the chance of a better life. Those with an adventurous spirit headed off in dangerous directions if they got a whiff of gold in the air. Sixty thousand people died in the late nineteenth century chasing dreams of gold in Dawson City when it became known that gold deposits had been found in the Klondike River of the Yukon territory in Canada. So many people had tenacious hopes of finding an answer to their hardships that they were willing to travel huge distances for the chance to improve their lot. News of the find reached the USA in July 1897 setting off the Klondike stampede. The sudden influx of people to the area threatened to cause a famine and the Canadian Mounties had to enforce a law that only travellers carrying over a year's supply of food would be allowed into the area. An entire city eventually grew up in the region and it was said that there were, 'strange things done in the midnight sun by the men who moil for gold . . .' (The Cremation of Sam McGee).

Yes, gold has certainly always been sought after and its future looks just as bright. It has more than doubled in price since 2001 when it was $277 an ounce and has now reached a new record at $950 per ounce. At the time of writing, gold is sitting on a twenty-five year high, and the weak dollar, high oil prices and global economic concern will continue to fuel the rise. I believe there's still a long way to go in this market because:

- There is an increase in demand from countries like India and China emerging as significant business nations with increasing wealth and seeking physical assets

- Gold has many uses in technology; technology has only one way to go and that's up, up, up

- Investors see gold as a safe option

- Gold prospectors still travel many parts of the world seeking deposits in rocks or stream beds and they are generally allowed to carry on their business undisturbed provided they work individually. In the US, panners are permitted provided that no explosives or machinery is used, and in the UK permission must be sought from landowners before a gold hunt can go ahead. But let me save you the trouble of getting your toes wet – the easiest way to join the gold rush is via the Stock Exchange

- Gold is now viewed as a mainstream investment and it's clear to see why. It is no longer reserved for only the wealthy to invest in and it offers security to investors. Its limited supply ensures its popularity. Although it is easily produced and clearly identifiable, it remains difficult to find; a one ounce golden nugget is rarer than a five carat diamond. Since its discovery it is believed that only 88,000 tons of gold have been taken from the earth, all of which could be compressed into an 18 yard cube. Far more is yet to be discovered. It is estimated that in every cubic mile of seawater there are 25 tons of gold, and the entire world's oceans conceal a staggering 10 billion tons. It is the scarcity that shrouds gold in mystery and secures continuing worldwide lust for it.

- The World Gold Council (WGC) released figures confirming the increasing popularity of gold. The demand during the last quarter of 2007 was $20.7 billion US dollars, a 30 per cent increase on demand for the same period in 2006. According to James Burton, the WGC's CEO, 'It is clear that gold's safe haven and hedging characteristics have been a major attraction for investors during this period of instability, greater inflationary fears and a falling dollar.'

Gold has many uses apart from being used for jewellery and trinkets including:

- As metal conductors in circuits, satellite reflectors and stereo connectors
- Dental fillings as early as 700 BC
- Radioactive gold is used in diagnosis for certain medical conditions
- Gold has the highest malleability of any metal. This means that gold is used for sheets of only millionths of an inch thick known as gold leaf.

The USA, not surprisingly, has the largest gold reserves but the country producing the most gold in the world is South Africa, producing over a billion dollars of gold each year, followed by Canada at around £60 million. The USA is the third largest producer. China and India are extremely important buyers of gold, as an emerging business population with increased wealth look to invest in physical assets.

Silver is another precious metal with many uses other than decorative:

- Since William Conrad Roentgen's discovery that x-rays activate silver halide crystals, medical diagnosis has been revolutionized and since just 2002 radiographic use of silver has consumed 90 million troy ounces globally

- One in every seven pairs of US prescription glasses incorporates silver melted into the glass; it helps to block 97 per cent of the sun's ultraviolet rays

- Silver contacts are used for the contacts in electrical circuits

- Jet engines that power modern aircraft use silver in high-performance bearings – also used by Rolls Royce

Even if the demand for silver in the fashion industry

declines it is clear to see that the need for it will increase in technology terms. In 2005, 409.3 million ounces of silver were consumed in industry and only 249.6 million ounces by the jewellery and silverware markets. Over 164.8 million ounces were used by the photographic sector.

Silver is also highly undervalued and the demand for precious metals in general has seen the price of silver bounce back from over 100 years of lower prices. Even investors such as Bill Gates are getting in on the act with a $10 million investment into Pan American silver, a silver mining company. Mexico produces the most silver in the West.

Despite the continuing popularity of gold and silver, diamonds are considered by many to be the ultimate representation of wealth. They are an investment that can be transported physically. Some very famous people have invested in diamonds; Charlotte Church for example is well known for purchasing shiny big stones.

Coloured diamonds are a particularly sound investment. Over the past ten years, 24 out of the 25 highest prices paid at auction houses for gemstones were for the coloured diamonds. I believe that the long-term potential for investing in diamonds looks rosy, stronger perhaps than ever before.

There are many colours and they are classified according to their rarity:

- Extremely rare: blue, green, violet, red
- Rare: olive, pink, white, orange
- Fairly rare: brown, black, yellow, grey, colourless

Extremely rare diamonds only appear on the market a handful of times a year. An investment in diamonds is a medium- to long-term venture of at least five years or more.

For investors who are happy to face bigger risks, the liquidity of the futures market offers a healthy potential for growth. Even palladium and uranium are traded on the New York Mercantile Exchange, and investors in mining stocks are reaping the benefits of a 'super cycle' in natural resources which will of course have ups and downs but long term will produce exciting returns for many years to come.

The current commodities super cycle is being driven by demand from the industrialization of emerging markets. Meanwhile, shortages of equipment are constraining the launch of new mining projects, driving up costs and limiting supply. Join me on the next step to add another string to your bow as we investigate the world of other commodities.

STEP 30

ENTER A BRAVE NEW WORLD

We cannot become what we need to be by remaining what we are.
Max Depree

Trade and the world will be your oyster. Exploit the developing world and watch the readies roll in. The process of making a mint by taking a cut from the purchase and sale of goods has long since been part of human history. When Christopher Columbus set sail in 1492 and 'discovered' America he was actually intending to get rich by trade. Becoming an infamous but penniless explorer was not on his original agenda.

Interwoven in the fabric of human history has been a desire to discover and conquer the world. Trade has inspired many adventurous entrepreneurs to head off in perilous new directions and uncharted territory. The risks undertaken on these expeditions were unknown to the traders and by no means slim. Impassable routes, stormy seas and bandits lying in wait prepared to slit throats for a piece of booty, meant the journey to rich rewards was often extremely hazardous.

In this day and age you don't even have to leave the

comfort of your own armchair; that's the beauty of global trade in the twenty-first century. But trading can still be a thrill, and the human appetite for thrill has made (and lost) many a personal fortune.

There have always been surpluses in one part of the world and deficits elsewhere and there still are. The trick to becoming a successful trader is to find out what they are and become the middleman between the two. With the rise of the markets in countries like India, China and Russia the opportunities for trade are abounding. In business terms there is still a wealth of uncharted territory in these lands and windows of opportunity waiting to be opened that perhaps only remain ajar in the Western world. I'm not saying there aren't still opportunities all over the world, but they're harder to exploit in countries where the markets are very well developed.

So what are commodities? We have already looked at the glittery shinny side, but the real trade happens with items we use every day that make our world go round. Take a look at the list below, all of which can be bought and sold. The easy way to do so is within a unit trust where the fund manager looks after the investment decisions for you (see Step 32).

- Copper
- Aluminium
- Soya beans
- Zinc
- Nickel
- Lead
- Sugar
- Cotton
- Coffee
- Cocoa
- Natural gas
- Crude oil
- Heating oil
- Cattle
- Wheat
- Red wheat
- Water
- Alternative energy
- Fibres
- Corn

Commodities are seen as a very good investment as the emerging markets need them to fuel their rapid growth. For example, trade between China and the African nations leapt by 39 per cent in 2005. It makes sense to capitalize on the growing trade of some of the world's fastest growing markets. If you have already established an enterprise, it may be that it would be suitable to grow your business overseas. Check out www.uktradeinvest.gov.uk for information on high growth markets.

If you currently have no ideas that you could trade worldwide you do not need to despair. You can invest in the new world by purchasing commodities either directly or as mentioned via unit trusts and still gain from the fast growing economies that currently make major shares in the UK look totally sluggish. It is likely to continue this way for some time so enjoy, make hay while the sun is shining!

Whether it's fine art you wish to trade or home made designer jewellery, it's simple to invest and tap into the international market.

STEP 31

TAKE A RISK

The policy of being too cautious is the greatest risk of all.
Jawaharlal Nehru (1889–1964), First Prime Minister of India

The ability to accept and embrace risk is what separates winners from losers. The level of risk you feel happy to take on is entirely personal and I can't give you a hard and fast rule for this step. Each person has a varying appetite for risk.

Years ago I visited in Cornwall the old ruins of a castle, which sat on the edge of a cliff over the sea. I climbed over one of the walls on this particularly windy day, edging along the 12 inch ledge on the cliffside just for the thrill of it and the feeling of achievement once I'd reached the safety of inside the castle walls.

Attitude to risk can alter over time – when I think of what I did back then I go cold; one slip would have meant certain death. Such a stupid risk to take, I can see that now. However, the experience does demonstrate two things: first (as mentioned), that the element of risk is a changing force; second, the power of confidence – I was cock-sure I wouldn't fall.

While I would suggest caution in the early stages of wealth-building it certainly pays to be a bit more speculative as your wealth begins to grow. Risk quite often spells reward. And, after all, for the purposes of this book, we are out for all we can get. We are in pursuit of wealth. Obviously your mortgage, household bills and comforts for children, etc., come first but if you're confident that you're in a position to take care of these first, then you can consider your risk level and begin to accumulate.

One method to use to help you decide the level of risk you are prepared to take is to do another quick stock take – calculate your income, outgoings, assets liability and then work out how much you are prepared to play with before you invest.

There are a number of ways to off-set the risks you take:

- Arm yourself with as much information about the invest-ment/venture BEFORE taking the plunge and seek independent advice

- Think about what would happen if you lost everything you invested in risk funds – if you can't afford to lose, it's not a risk worth taking!

- Consider whether you need short-, medium- or long-term returns on your money – is it the right investment for you?

- Are you comfortable with the level of risk? If you thrive on excitement, then high-risk ventures may be just what you need, but make sure you can sleep at night. If it's going to keep you awake, don't do it!

- DON'T PUT ALL YOUR EGGS IN ONE BASKET! Spread the risk

For some people risk doesn't spell danger; for them it just means that the outcome of an event is not set in stone. For others, risk means fear, insecurity and ultimately unhappiness. If that is the case for you, please stick to the basic rules of this book and prioritize your happiness and inner well-being. In other words hold fast to your wallet and walk in the other direction. And besides, there are other ways to make money that involve little or no risk.

I have a little game for you to try to find out what kind of person you are in terms of danger levels and risk taking. Are you cautious, cautious balanced, just in the middle, balanced/adventurous or damned right adventurous?

Take a look at the pyramid overleaf. The idea is that at the bottom of the pyramid where the base and foundation is very wide we have the safer way of building a portfolio, like cash under the mattress (if there was no risk of fire and theft). Then as we move further up the pyramid we find the riskier investments. Where do you find yourself? Halfway up maybe? Or right at the summit? It's possible of course to be at one point with an amount of your money and yet in a different place with the balance!

Climbing the pyramid takes you up the steps to success but you must choose wisely or you could slide back down. Begin at the bottom to build a secure base and then gradually add others from higher levels if you feel this suits your profile.

Assess how much you can afford to lose before taking the plunge and remember that the faster the gain, the riskier the venture. Always assess the risks. If you don't seriously consider your situation and your expectations, you might be disappointed. Try a small amount of money first and gradually increase your exposure to risk, banking profits along the way. Have a realistic monetary goal and when you arrive at that figure, bank it. Risks will decrease as your experience grows.

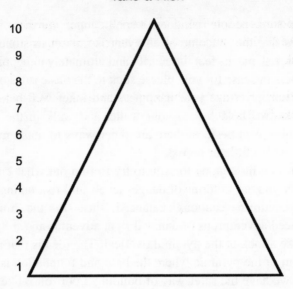

Fig. 3: Pyramid of risk

My pyramid of risk is 0–10 on the scale.

- Penny shares, gambling, commodities, spreadbetting and small companies listed on AIM (Alternative Investment Market) and any investment with an unproven track record – Risk 9/10

- Stocks and shares (in one company) – Risk 7/8

- Collective investments including unit and investment trusts and equity ISAs – Risk 5/6

- Insurance and investment bonds if invested in income funds (although varies greatly depending on the funds) – Risk 4/5

- Property including your main home – Risk 3/4

- Deposit-based building society accounts including cash ISAs (if there was no risk of a bank becoming insolvent) – Risk 1

- National Savings products as these are UK Government backed – Risk 0.5

STEP 32

EXTEND YOUR PORTFOLIO TO INCLUDE UNIT TRUSTS AND TRACKERS

Increased means and increased leisure are the two civilizers of man.
Benjamin Disraeli

You have reached a plateau, a safe haven, the calm before the storm. In this step you get to play with fire but with some protective clothing. You can taste a little excitement and be part of the action but dodge unnecessary risk. Interested? Then it's time you invested in a unit trust or tracker fund.

Unit trusts allow you to play a little with the market, dipping your big toe in the water but keeping the rest of you completely dry. In a couple of steps' time we'll explore ways to get the best out of the stock market as a personal investor but if, at the end of a long day (in the office/factory/shop/wherever!) you can think of nothing less appealing than getting to grips with investment jargon, unit trusts are the way forward. They will help immensely in your bid to be rich.

Unit trusts have fund managers (you know the ones who get the big bonuses) who collect all monies from private (i.e. you) or institutional investors, and then bulk buy shares in companies, gilts, bonds or a combination of all three. They can be UK based or overseas depending on the specific trust and because they have millions of pounds pooled together at their disposal they are in a position to call the shots in terms of negotiating deals, thereby maximizing their (and ultimately your) purchasing power. By pooling together with others you avoid the excessive cost of buying and selling shares in small amounts.

The value of your portfolio will change daily and you can sell part or all of your unit holding any time you wish. Obviously you are going to be charged for the privilege of having a management group make all the decisions for you and charges vary but usually the initial fee is 5 per cent and this is taken from the money you invest at the very start. This is often referred to as the Bid Offer spread, so, if you buy and sell in the same day you'll come away with 5 per cent less money in your pocket even if the price of the units were to stay the same. There is often an ongoing charge which is around 1 per cent per year which is paid for by selling units held in the fund.

Investment trusts are also available and are in the main lower charging than unit trusts. Investment trusts were launched back in 1868 but seem to be less popular despite the lower charges. This is possibly due to the split-capital scandal a few years ago when they were sold as 'safe' but this complex version was far from safe.

It is always important when investing to be open minded about charges. For example, to save, let's say, 0.5 per cent per year by way of a charge and invest in a poor performing investment is the height of folly. If you had invested £1,000 over the past year, the best performing fund would have given you a £394 profit while the worst performing fund a £468 loss!

The good news is that you have so many choices. You can invest in any country in the world and in all sectors. Below are a few examples.

- Area: UK   Sector: Healthcare
- Area: US   Sector: Banking
- Area: India   Sector: Small companies
- Area: Europe Sector: Emerging markets
- Area: Russia   Sector: New wealth
- And, in addition, commodities from any area in the world

As mentioned in Step 30 commodities, which can be purchased via a unit trust, are potentially very rewarding since the developing world will need to purchase massive amounts (oil, gas, etc) to continue with its rapid expansion.

As well as the many choices of geographical area and sector one of the most popular funds is the 'Tracker', so named because they do just that: they track the stock market's main indices. Again you can choose which index you wish to track. They exploded in popularity in the 1990s because they aim to beat the wider stock market. The down side (you knew there would be one!) is that sometimes they pick the wrong stocks in the indices and then they underperform. Research so far shows that in good times (known as a bull market) trackers perform well, while in falling markets (known as a bear market) they fall down the performance chart! Sound financial sense says they should be just part of an overall basket of investments.

A word of warning: even though investment and unit trusts are considered less risky than holding shares directly, there is still a risk that the fund could fall in value; any investment that has stocks and shares is not suitable for someone with a cautious profile – if you do not want to have a risk of being burnt, do not play with fire!

STEP 33

RAISE YOUR BETS

*Money is the seed of money, and the first guinea is sometimes
more difficult to acquire than the second million.*
Jean Jacques Rousseau

Want a half-way house? Then come and rest here a while. We
move on from the comfort of fund managers investing on your
behalf, but don't worry all you need is:

- Order
- Method
- Logic

as advocated by my alter ego, Hercule Poirot.

Initial financial outlay is minimal, the cost of a financial
paper, literally. And then it's up to you with investment in the
purchase of blue-chip shares. The potential returns are
outstanding. Read on to find out more.

Don't worry about being an investment novice. If you stick
to the system you should beat the market consistently and

systematically. Ready to take the plunge? Excellent! Firstly you'll need the *Financial Times* as you will find in there a list of the top 100 companies known as the FTSE 100. From this, draw up a list of the largest 30 companies, noting their dividend yield and share price. Then from these 30 companies, extract a list of the ten highest dividend yielding shares. If you invest in these shares, it is highly likely that you'll beat the market and that is quite a feat.

The system was devised by the American fund manager, Michael O'Higgins. You can read about his high-yield system in depth in *Beating the Dow* but basically it's very simple. His theory works in practice because over a long period, high yielding stocks, with dividends re-invested, have a powerful compound factor and have beaten the Dow Jones Industrial Average by a long way.

Adapted to the UK market the same system has produced equally impressive results, beating the market significantly. It is an excellent strategy to follow when you're a stock market virgin as it requires next to no knowledge and only moderate accounting skills.

The dividend yield of a company is calculated by expressing the annual dividend as a percentage of the share price. Let's say a sandwich bar company has a share price of 100p and pays 1.6p as a dividend, per share. This means that 1.6 per cent of the 100p share price represents the dividend or:

1.6/100p x 100 = 1.6 per cent

If the company suddenly took a nosedive and the share price fell to 50p the yield would rise to 3.2 per cent, assuming the dividend continued at the same level, and the share would then become a high yielder. Since it's bad PR for companies to reduce their dividends, the directors are often reluctant to do that, so at least for a while you should benefit from a high yielding share with the prospect of good capital growth!

Risks are lower than investing in some other companies because those you invest in are of such a size that they are less likely to experience a monumental crisis. Yet shares with high yields are not the current favourites of investors.

This is good news for you. It means that when the popularity of the stock returns (as inevitably happens with the circle of the stock markets) you, as an investor, enjoy double benefits: the rising share price plus a relatively high income in the interim. These combined effects can make high yielders awesome in terms of wealth building potential.

Over the long term the true wealth of a company will be reflected by its share price but in the short term it's merely a balance between buyers and sellers. All you're doing when picking out high yielders of the blue-chip companies is benefiting from the natural peaks and troughs in the market. As Warren Buffett, the world's most successful investor said, 'In the short term the market is a voting machine but in the long run it is a weighing machine.'

STEP 34

SPECULATE TO ACCUMULATE

The optimist sees opportunity in every danger;
the pessimist sees danger in every opportunity.
Winston Churchill

If you examine the performance of UK shares over the last century you may feel compelled to become part of history and invest. Many consider alternative investments first but they still cannot resist. Are you ready to join them in their expedition?

Now, before we start we need a team talk. As we climb this step I want you to make sure you 'look before you leap' because investing in stocks and shares is a volatile pastime. I'm not trying to dissuade you; shares have great potential and in the long term are likely to provide excellent growth. What I am saying is proceed with caution.

To play the markets you have to accept that there will be risks. In 1973 the value of shares fell by 29 per cent with worse yet to come. The year after, speculators had to bear the brunt of a shocking 52 per cent decline in the market. In 1975 shares surged by 152 per cent. In other words it's volatile out there. There are no guarantees and no quick fixes. If you aim to pay off debts by banking on a successful year on the market, forget it; it's not for the short term. Be prepared to leave your investment alone because the fact is that shares will out-perform almost any other investment, but only if left alone for the long term.

In basic terms the way to play the stock market and win is to buy low and sell high, that's the long and the short of it – simple isn't it? The answer is no, not always. There is an art to knowing what to buy and when and to knowing when to sell. Inevitably there is also an element of timing involved. However, since the number of books written filled with advice for success on the markets would fill my office I will avoid going into too many complexities here and limit my advice to some basic common sense rules that will set you on your way!

Investing in stocks and shares is a form of gambling as there is a risk involved. However, by studying the companies you are considering investing in, their performance, probability of future successes and share price you can greatly reduce the risk.

One of the first tricks of winning in the market is to try to develop a nose for the task. To sniff out the type of stocks that you think will appeal to other investors. If you buy some shares in a company that you think will appeal to investors in the short-term or long-term future, then you know that at some point someone is going to be willing to pay good money for them. That's what makes playing the market such an intriguing game; speculating the future and profiting when you get it right.

I strongly advise a trial period to try to get into the psychology of it. Observe the movements in the market and keep a dummy portfolio of shares you think you would be likely to buy. Try this over, say, a four- to six-month period and see how profitable you would have been had you been playing for real. Keep a note of the type of shares that were successful and work out why. See the mass psychology in action when panic sets in and investors copy each other like sheep.

If you like the odd dabble but don't want huge risks, then it's best to buy shares in things you are familiar with or at least understand slightly. If you are a techno-whiz, for example, and understand computer technology and that particular market, then investing in a company that invents or manufactures components that you feel will take off in the future should be a good buy.

Buying what you know is a good basic rule to follow as you're much more likely to be in a position to predict future demands on the product/company if you understand the market it's in. You are much less likely to be puzzled by slick marketing ploys and unrealistic forecasts of future profits if you are in the know.

Bear in mind there is a certain seductive pull towards the 'mysterious' stocks which can lead you to stake a whole lot more than is really sensible, placing all your hopes in little more than a glamorous name. Over-optimism can be deadly. Be positive, confident and timely but don't be daft!

Whilst on the subject of being daft . . . one of my other golden rules is to make sure that you base your reasons for investing in a company on shrewd, well thought-out business principles, not on a whim or as a favour to someone or perhaps because of a deeply held conviction; investing in an organic food company simply because you are passionate about organic food is only sensible if rational, well-considered market analysis reveals that the industry will keep on thriving and the company is a good sound bet. Buying with your heart can lead to trouble if other factors are not examined as well.

Building a portfolio of shares can be immensely satisfying and a great source of fun. Once you have a portfolio established you have a ready-made second income from dividends or you could choose to have these reinvested to increase your shareholding and therefore future capital growth.

Hopefully your mindset at this stage in the book is that you want to use the money you've accumulated thus far to really start to work for you. Investing in shares can, as mentioned, be fun. I don't mean that it's fun because you don't take the whole matter seriously but it's fun to research the market and choose where it's best to place your money.

As I've said before, money generates more money. By transforming the money you have into an asset (i.e. shares or investments of some sort, property, etc) you can create an income stream and a long-term reward. I see stocks and shares as a solid and wise choice for investment because, despite the possibility of prices decreasing, overall, over the long term, investment in shares outperforms most other asset classes.

Try to develop an understanding of the market and grasp the basic jargon used. Knowledge of how shares work is useful as is a basic understanding of company accounts and how to interpret them. A good stockbroker will help and advise you and will act as an agent when buying and selling stocks. However, even the experts find it difficult to predict where the stock market is heading. The most important point to remember when dealing with shares is to select intelli-gently!

Reading is an important tool for the successful investor, and one of the most vital daily reads is the excellent *Financial Times*, with the weekly *Investors Chronicle* following closely. The weekend edition of the FT summarizes the weekly movements in the market and provides up-to-date business news which may be of significance to your portfolio. *The Economist*, published weekly, is a very useful magazine for providing an international picture on events shaping the world. Then the monthly publication, *Money Management* (FT business magazine) provides investors with essential financial statistics of most UK funds including unit and investment trust and insurance companies' funds.

Speculating on the market has nothing to do with feelings or intuition. If you decide to invest in something because you like the name of the company or get a tingle when you think about it, then I suggest you abandon the idea now. You won't need a crystal ball to become successful in the stock market. What you will need to do is study the shares available, the current climate, future needs, etc. Leave star gazing to dreamers. My aim is to make your dreams a reality.

In summary then:

- Don't follow the crowd; use sound research to make any decisions
- Buy the right stocks at the right price
- Don't be fooled by 'proven' techniques and technical analysis
- Invest in things you understand
- Buy with your head, not your heart

And, remember: the price you're willing to pay for a stock should be based more on what future speculators will be prepared to pay for it, rather than the stripped down bare bones value of the company. Any item, thing, object, property, business, stock, is only worth the value someone else is willing to credit it with.

If only one could invest in hindsight, with this in our locker we would play such a good game, always winning our bets on the stock market fairground!

STEP 35

LOOK TO THE LONG TERM

*It's good to have money and the things that money can buy, but it's
good, too, to check up once in a while and make sure that you
haven't lost the things that money can't buy.*
George Horace Lorimer

We've looked at a number of ways to invest, either in
property, investments or in the stock market. Now all you
have to do is appreciate and acknowledge one of the most
important investment rules: investments are generally for the
long term. Very few people manage to catapult themselves
into immediate prosperity. The rest of us keep plugging
away and get there over a prolonged period of determined
effort.

The unwelcome truth, as we saw in Step 26, is that 'get rich
quick' schemes often end in disaster. The only assured way of
reaching your bounty is by following your dream with
persistence and a good old bulldog spirit.

• Be bold
• Be strong

- Be staunch in spirit
- Be PATIENT!

Also remember never to panic. Keep your beady eye on things. Allow time for your money to grow. You won't get rich by making weak decisions and frittering good money away on early redemption and penalty charges unless there is very good reason; also selling shares at the wrong time because they were purchased on a whim or lack of initial research is riding down a wrong way street!

An investment of any kind carries risk but those risks can be minimized drastically by investing in a broad range of products and only using money you are likely not to need for a period of time.

As I've already said, we do need short-term investments for money needed, say, for an unforeseen emergency. You never can tell when you might be in need of liquid cash to pull you out of an immediate fix. We've already covered the best options for money you may need in a hurry – remember in Step 12?

Medium- to long-term investments are those you would expect to deliver returns in the next five to fifteen years.

There are a range of options available and Table 8 will help you to choose which type of investment best suits your own personal preferred time trail. You already know what type of risk-taker you are from playing the game in Step 31.

It is a great idea to build a family of investments that match your risk level and work in harmony with your time trail to help develop financial security. You need, ideally, to protect against deflation and build a portfolio that builds long-term wealth.

I always recommend taking advice when the risk is high with an investment. Don't forget nowadays it's not just the risk of the fund going up or down but the security of where

Table 8: Comparison of investments

Investment	Asset type	Time trail	Always should take advice?
Cash ISA	Deposit based investment	Instant	No
Premium bonds	National Savings product	3 months	No
Bank and building society accounts	Deposit based investment	Instant or stated notice period	No
Fixed interest rate bonds	Can be both deposit and equity based!	5 years plus	Yes
Equity ISAs	Stocks and shares	5 years plus	Yes
Unit and investment trusts	Equities including any specialist funds	5 years plus	Yes
Insurance bonds	Various assets including equities	5 years plus	Yes
Single company shares	Stocks and shares	3–5 years or if you reach your dream price before	Yes

your money is invested. Will the bank still be there with your money in two years' time? Most people investing in deposit accounts in the UK since the credit crunch are quite rightly not so worried about a small percentage loss in interest if they can be sure of the financial security side of things.

If purchasing shares right now there are some great bargains to be had thanks to the credit crunch; markets have fallen. My 'in' phase is 'the 90 per cent club'. These are shares that have lost 90 per cent of their value in the last year. Building companies, for instance, who would be worth more than their current share price even if they simply closed shop and sold off all their land they own (called land-bank). These shares will turn right around soon so watch for the signs, study the price and Buy Buy BUY. For sure in any financial bad time, a million can be both lost or won!

Don't play the short game. Have patience and stay in it for the long haul. Your pertinacity will reap significant rewards; make sure you are a winner!

STEP 36

QUIT WHEN YOU'RE AHEAD

Nothing astonishes men more than common sense
and plain dealing.
Ralph Waldo Emerson

I don't mean you've made enough money, now stop. That's certainly not the case. Now that you've started to move towards prosperity you must get slicker and quicker and focus, focus, focus.

Real wealth comes from hard slog and application of a strong and well thought-out strategy and some financial know-how, learnt or borrowed. Get rich quick schemes don't work. If it sounds too good to be true, then it is too good to be true. There's no such thing as a free lunch, etc. To become rich you need to have a finger in lots of pies and you need investments that work for you, even while you sleep.

What I do mean when I say, 'quit when you're ahead' is that you need to learn to recognize when you'd be better off pulling out of a project, business or investment and taking your cash elsewhere.

I know I have said that long-term plans and investments

need to be left alone to grow. Stocks and shares, property and most financial investments don't make a fortune overnight and so you must invest and then leave well alone until they've grown. BUT, having said that, it is SO important to learn when to pull the plug and walk away. Don't we all wish that the great Muhammad Ali had quit when he was at the top of his sport? I will give you tips on recognizing when it's time to cut your losses and run. Throwing good money after bad is always a bad idea; there is an art to knowing when to stop.

So how do you recognize when it's time to turn your back on an investment?

Signs that you may be better off moving your money are:

- There has been a downturn in the market sector in which you are invested with little prospect of improvement for the foreseeable future, while other sectors are on the up!

- The investment has been limping since day one and remains sluggish with no positive news on the horizon

- You thought it would become popular but it's now 'old hat' or it's reached a peak and is on a definite downturn

- You've had to throw good money after bad and are tempted to do so again

- A scandal breaks with the company you hold shares with and the long-term future seems grim due to the adverse publicity

- If a company signals a profit warning, quick action could mean selling before the shares nose dive; good advice from an expert here is the key!

If you have invested in something that you totally understand (perhaps in your line of work) the signs will clearly be there for you to see.

Knowing when to quit is as important a part of becoming successful as knowing when and what to buy. Master this completely and riches certainly await you in this fast new world!

PART FOUR

BEING RICH

STEP 37

DEVELOP WAYS TO COPE WITH BEING THE RICHEST AROUND

Waste your money and you're only out of money,
but waste your time and you've lost a part of your life.
Michael LeBoeuf

I know it sounds ridiculous and you're probably yelling, 'Paul, if only I had problems like this, I would cope no sweat!' but being rich really can be problematic (problems that many would envy but nevertheless which may cause the rich to lose sleep). If you can afford to fork out £12,500 a year you can discuss some or all of these problems with like-minded people *suffering* similar wealth issues by joining the Tiger 21 club (The Investment Group for Exceptional Returns). To join you must have £5m in investable assets as a minimum. Membership of the club allows super-rich Americans to discuss not only investment strategies but also other worries peculiar only to the mega-rich.

One of our British equivalents is the Supper Club, an elite

dating society for which you have to run a business worth £1 million plus. Prospective members attend introductory evenings and, if they make the grade, their name is added to the guest list of some of the most exclusive parties in London where they are introduced to members of the opposite sex who are equally as affluent as themselves.

Over the last ten years since women have achieved so much more and reached higher places than ever before, their demands have become ever more complicated. Successful women are uninterested in the contents of a man's wallet. They seek someone who is attuned to their lifestyle and don't want to waste their precious time away from the boardroom on men who don't make the grade.

If people have spent much of their free time building a successful career or business, they often want to find others of like mind who have done the same thing. Sticking with those who have achieved success helps to cushion the wealthy from sometimes outright condemnation from those who aren't. The rich are often profoundly criticized while at the same time secretly admired. Wealth is often hated yet most people are compelled to lust after it.

Sigmond Freud taught that anyone who goes to such efforts to accumulate wealth is abnormal, with a pathological drive. He speculated that people who have a love of money were like children who play with their faeces and concluded, 'the most extensive connections seem to be those existing between the apparently so disparate complexes of defecation and interest in money'.

It's not easy for society to recover from that kind of analysis. The nineteenth century writer, Honoré de Balzac, a man who remained in debt for his entire life, coined the phrase, 'Behind every great fortune there is a crime'. The rich suffer from the deeply ingrained negative attitudes of the masses passed through the generations, from the days of King

Midas, who turned everything into gold at the mere touch. He turned his own daughter into gold, leaving future generations with the suggestion that, not only do riches prevent happiness, they actually destroy your life.

The good news is that it is quite possible to be rich, responsible and happy! But developing coping strategies is important because having more money than anyone you know can sometimes go to your head and that can get ugly. So make sure you handle your money well and your attitude even more carefully. The British value self-depreciation over most things. Mentioning your wealth or the value of things you own is tacky; don't be tempted to do it. Remaining tight-lipped about your fortune, especially to the taxman (LOL, I jest!) encourages admiration rather than resentment.

Being a custodian of wealth requires all the qualities that you've hopefully acquired in your quest for success in business: discretion, honesty, respect for others and consideration. Steer off course to your peril; you'll lose the respect of all who surround you.

It is so important to keep your feet firmly on the ground. Don't lose the common touch and isolate yourself from people who live in the 'real' world. Having said that, I'm not surprised that some wealthy people barricade themselves away; many do it to avoid being bombarded with requests for a hand-out. This can come from close relatives, friends, employees, acquaintances, distant neighbours, anyone. I say ugly because it is uncomfortable for everyone when this happens. Borrowing from friends and family is always a bad idea. It usually ends up with resentment and jeopardizes the best of relationships. It's partly the reason why some wealthy individuals end up living the life of a recluse. But we don't want you to go there. One of the fail-safes is to stay close to the people who love you or know you well or both – old friends, people who knew and liked you before you obtained wealth. They won't hound you to make their life better (you may be generous to these people anyway but real friends won't expect it).

If you find saying 'no' excruciatingly embarrassing, an excellent tactic to use is to refer the 'beggar' to your financial adviser or accountant. Most people will be very reluctant to approach anyone else with their request and at least you won't have to face the die-hard ones that do. It makes sense that you would refer proposals to an adviser and so it saves embarrassment all round. My wealthy clients have referred requests from the determined to me and I have politely informed them that the money is 'tied up' and there is no ready cash. Of course, there may be occasions when you want to say 'yes' but it still makes sense to keep it official.

Begging letters from the 'have-nots' are just one of a number of problems encountered by the people who have. It is certainly true that it takes a monumental effort and years of hard work to become truly rich but, once you get there, happiness and contentment are not guaranteed. As with most things in life, it pays to be prepared. Many people find coping with money extremely difficult, but if you are aware of the difficulties you may encounter with new-found wealth and try to anticipate how you may feel, you can develop strategies to cope with them. It is wise to develop the skills while you're still climbing or you could find you reach the top and then have no idea what to do when you get there.

Psychologists say that their rich patients are 'emotionally different'; they don't worry about the things that bug most people in their daily lives such as mortgage payments and the high cost of living and so they suffer other afflictions. The level of choice available to the wealthy can cause as much frustration as not having enough to make ends meet or, as Émile Durkheim explains, 'the less limited one feels, the more intolerable all limitation appears'.

Along with a wealth of new choices, the rich can spend far too many precious hours worrying about the possibility of losing it all and I can understand why; when you have it all, you have so much to lose!

While on a plane back from Luxembourg recently with Chris an important client of mine (and now friend), age 47, whom I was advising on the best home for some of his self-made fortune, I asked the following question: 'Are you truly content with your lot?' He smiled and replied: 'I feel I should be but I am not! If I were content, I feel the race would be over and that the end would be close. Contentment is for when I am in my 80s.' I have to say I totally agree.

This confirms that there is no measure of when someone should 'feel wealthy' and money itself does not bring content-ment. It does, however, bring comfort and that's surely worth every penny!

Having lots of money is a position, a stage, but does not mean you're any better at making financial decisions. Therefore a cool head and logical decisions are needed when you have money just as much as they are required when building the foundation to your goal. Building wealth is hard work but is very well paid! It's worth the struggle for all those who achieved or they would have stopped in their quest, and yes it does bring certain problems but has many com-pensations to oil the wheels.

STEP 38

PASS YOUR WEALTH ON TO THOSE YOU LOVE

Most people save all their lives and leave it to somebody else.
Hedy Lamarr

When you go, you go alone and with nothing. You leave the world just as you arrived: naked, with money being useless. It's the old adage 'you can't take it with you' and however frustrating it may be there's not a thing you can do about it. Or is there?

Well for starters you can make sure you enjoy every minute of being wealthy and never lose sight of the fact that you are its temporary custodian. It's sensible to work on strategies that will ease the hassle when you pass your money onto surviving relatives so that they can enjoy it too. Substantial estates can cause a number of problems and take an age to resolve unless the will has been carefully planned. When families are left reeling with the grief of losing a loved one, the last thing they want is to worry about tax as a result of poor planning and a will that's not watertight and comprehensive. And it's not a good idea to leave it until you're dribbling in your old-folks home to sort out matters. I will show you all the tricks and tips to pass on your wealth with as few headaches as possible for your family. I know it may grate a little to think about a time when you won't be around to enjoy the profits of your hard work but it's important to make plans.

And, after all, it's not such an unpalatable problem to have, is it? Working out who to leave the abundance of wealth you've accumulated to . . . Well, actually, you'd be surprised at the headaches this 'problem' can cause. OK, I agree that it's better to have to worry about it than have nothing to leave behind you except for a big overdraft but it's not just aristocrats who have to worry about it these days.

The global economic boom of the past decade has created private fortunes on an unprecedented scale. The number of millionaires in Britain has spiralled over the last ten years and they're not all lottery winners. The number of British people with investable assets of $1 million or more grew by 8 per cent last year to a total of 485,000 according to a study by Capgemini and Merrill Lynch. In the USA there are now more than 9 million households that are worth more than $1 million or more and the number of households worth $10 million or $25 million has also doubled. The increase in wealth in Britain alone has risen astonishingly over the past thirty years.

Many of the new rich are professional people who have worked with determination over a prolonged period – doctors, lawyers, perhaps even builders who have had the means to start their own company. The majority of these people are dealing with issues that were unheard of in their own ancestry and so they can't go to their parents for the answer. They may have an overabundance of assets but they lack the knowledge needed to deal with matters of prosperity.

Not only do most people not want to lose the fortunes they've amassed or see them pass into the hands of the Government, they also most certainly don't want their kids to become spoilt brats with no need or desire to go out and conquer their own little piece of the world. How much is enough to leave them? Enough to secure them a stress-free future but not so much that you screw up their chances of living a normal life!

Assuming you amass a large sum that you consider a corrupting influence on your children's future, there are ways to avoid giving them too much, too soon.

It is possible to create trust funds accessible only when they reach a certain age or lump-sum allowances given at fixed terms. Setting aside lump sums for important milestones in their life is a good idea, i.e. for a car, house, or investment in a business. Even then I don't think it's a good idea to tell them about it before you bestow it on them – how demotivating to know that you'll get a huge lump sum at age 25 to buy a house; would you bother working hard after leaving full-time education if you knew that was coming? Of course, it would be better to witness some effort on their part to make their own way. Some families like to encourage their children to develop empathy for others and so establish their own family charity in the hope that their children will continue where they leave off. In America it has become known as 'giving while living' and their considerable tax benefits for charitable donations have encouraged the super-rich to share their wealth around still further.

The world's richest man, the American Warren Buffet, further encouraged the trend when he donated at least £15 billion to charity in 2006 rather than leave any more to his children. Our own Simon Cowell reckons on donating his entire fortune, estimated at around £100 million, to his dogs, (crazy I know!). But you don't have to resort to making your poodle the richest canine in England, unless that is what you prefer of course.

If the hairs on the back of your neck stand up at the thought of handing 40 per cent of the wealth you've worked so hard to accrue to the taxman, then read on. There are ways to counter the balance and it doesn't have to be a headache.

Inheritance Tax (IHT) is another name for Estate Duty, first levied in the 1880s. It is a tax on the wealth you pass on when you die. Obviously you don't want the good old Inland Revenue to be a major beneficiary to all the wealth you will have created by the time it's your turn to leave the earth and so it makes sense to make plans early on.

The good news is we are currently all allowed to leave an estate of £312k without paying tax. However due to the rise in house prices over the past 20 years, this limit is completely busted by many estates. This, in turn, led to pressure on the Chancellor to take action. Therefore in his pre-budget report in 2007, he announced that the unused Inheritance Tax nil rate band (£312k) on the first death of a spouse or civil partner could be carried forward for the surviving spouse or partner. This applies to all deaths on or after 9 October 2007 no matter when the first spouse or partner died.

So we have established that a married couple or civil partnership can now pass on £624k without paying IHT which stands at a whooping 40 per cent of any excess. For estates with more than this, don't panic. We just have a little more planning to do! See my tips on IHT planning below.

- Ask your pension provider for a nomination form – this should ensure that the money stays outside your estate on your death

- You can gift assets, money or property to your children; this starts the clock ticking on a Potentially Exempt Transfer (PET) which means that, should you live seven years, the money will be deemed as outside your estate; in fact, the tax bill reduces after year 3 to year 7. However, remember the tale about King Lear: he gifted his kingdom to his daughters and they repaid him by throwing him out!

* Everyone has a annual allowance of £3,000 and we all can give small gifts up to £250 to any one person

* We can all give gifts on marriage; parents can give £5,000, grandparents £2,500 and anyone else £1,000 to the happy couple

* Shares that are purchased on the Alternative Investment Market (AIM) and held for two years are free from IHT on death; this index is full with small UK companies (powering companies of tomorrow) and the Government is encouraging investment in this area. Take advice as not all AIM listed companies qualify!

* Trusts can be written which help with IHT planning. They are used often in conjunction with an investment; seek independent financial advice

So it's not as bad as it seemed at first. The list above is not exhaustive and good planning really does go a long way. I know it's unpleasant to think about the subject of your departure from the earth but it really is a job that needs doing. Bite the bullet and make plans now; nothing grates the family you leave behind quite as much as a poorly considered or, worse still, absent will. You don't really want to run the risk of relatives scrapping for their portion of your wealth while you're pushing up the daisies do you?

Another alternative is to spend the bloody lot before you go and enjoy! You might save yourself a very big posthumous tax-bill.

STEP 39

ENJOY!

I cannot, truly I cannot, sit in a chair all day reflecting how truly admirable I am.
Hercule Poirot

You've done what you set out to do. You've amassed a fortune or at the very least achieved financial security. You've worked your fingers to the bone and now it's time to enjoy it all.

I know, I know, throughout the book I've encouraged you to chant mantras and I've berated those who rest on their laurels if they are not happy with their lot. A rolling stone gathers no moss and all that stuff. But there comes a time when you need to enjoy even while still moving forward. This step is all about enjoying the life you've dreamed about and created for yourself. You reached out to grab for it, now make the most of it.

And don't make the mistake of measuring what you've achieved in cash terms. It's a selfish world out there but there are far more important measures of the time you spent on the climb. I hope that you have remained close to those you love.

If not, it's not too late to repair it now. I hope you've had fun, been fair to those you've employed and perhaps generous to some people you don't even know!

Building wealth is an exciting and speckled quest; enjoying the profits of your labour a rewarding, long-lasting adventure. Spending time with family and friends is so valuable and you've earned enough by now to take the time to spend with those important to you. You set out with a goal of becoming rich and once you've achieved that you can live a rich life, a life full of variety and spice, love and friendship.

Think about the things you've always wanted to do. Places you've never seen, experiences you've never had the time or money to indulge in. Make the climb worthwhile. You will hopefully, through your efforts, be in a position to buy most things you desire. You will have access to the world's most precious treasures.

Spend wisely though – one wealthy individual lined bar stools of his yacht with the soft foreskins from sperm-whale penises. If, like me, you find that hard to understand, a little ostentatious one may say, then use the products of your climb to help others who haven't been in a position even to make the first step.

Deciding on how best to help a cause you feel strongly about requires some careful thinking. Some global charities require a bottomless pit and it can seem like putting your money into a black-hole. Smaller charities closer to home might be a better choice and, if you've backed off on the work front, you may even want to devote some free time to get involved in some of their work. Experience of business is invaluable in some organizations and you might be just what they're looking for.

One of my goals is to give someone a chance who hasn't found life a piece of cake thus far. I intend to find someone

who has been on the thin end and put him or her in a
position to get into business (similar to the film *Trading
Places* staring Eddie Murphy). I feel that with the right
opportunity many people have the drive and skill set to
succeed.

Signing off

That's me done for now. I've passed on all the advice I am
able to and I dearly hope that I've helped you, in some small
way, to achieve your dream of becoming rich. Maybe you're
not quite there yet and, if not, please stick with it. Keep
following the path you mapped out for yourself in Step 6 and
don't deviate from it.

I also hope that you've enjoyed the time you've spent
reading this book and perhaps gleaned more from these
pages than written words of financial advice. Enjoy putting
your ideas into practice. I have been very lucky in that I love
what I do and have enjoyed every minute of my climb
towards success. I truly hope you gain as much pleasure
from the struggle towards your goal as I have. After all, 'in
the end, it's not the years in your life that count. It's the
life in your years,' as Abraham Lincoln would have it. And
who am I to argue? I'm just a poor boy from Clapham who
clung to his dreams and didn't let go until they became
reality.

You may have decided, after reading this book, that you
don't want great wealth after all, that the prize at the end is not
worth the race. It's difficult to judge what wealth is anyway.
How much must a person own before he or she is considered
wealthy? One million, perhaps ten? I don't think it's possible
to put a price on someone's head, a marker of rich or not quite
rich. If you ask me, 'Who is rich?', I say, 'Anyone who thinks
they are.'

Visit www.paulbanfield.co.uk and let me know your goal, or if you have reached your star already, I would truly like to know you achieved it.

INDEX

To order these Right Way titles please fill in the form below

No. of copies	Title	Price	Total
	Going Self-Employed	£5.99	
	Successful Property Letting	£9.99	
	Internet Marketing	£7.99	
	For P&P add £2.50 for the first book, £1 for each additional book		
	Grand Total		**£**

Name: _____

Address:_____

_____ Postcode: _____

Daytime Tel. No./Email_____
(in case of query)

Three ways to pay:
1. Telephone the TBS order line on 01206 255 800.
   Order lines are open Monday – Friday, 8:30am–5:30pm.
2. I enclose a cheque made payable to **TBS Ltd** for £_____
3. Please charge my ☐ Visa ☐ Mastercard ☐ Amex
   ☐ Maestro (issue no. _____)

Card number:_____

Expiry date: _____ Last three digits on back of card:_____

Signature: _____

(your signature is essential when paying by credit or debit card)

**Please return forms to Cash Sales/Direct Mail Dept.,
The Book Service, Colchester Road, Frating Green,
Colchester CO7 7DW.**

Enquiries to readers@constablerobinson.com.

Constable and Robinson Ltd (directly or via its agents)
may mail, email or phone you about promotions or products.

☐ Tick box if you do not want these from us ☐ or our subsidiaries.

**www.right-way.co.uk
www.constablerobinson.com**